To my darling wife, Linda, and my son, Jeremy, whose love, encouragement and advice made it possible. It took a year out of all our lives, and I hope that the finished book is worth their sacrifices.

Acknowledgements

I have discussed the book with many friends and colleagues over the year, who generously gave me their comments. Of these I would thank particularly Victoria Reeves, John Knight, Geoffrey Spencer, Derrick Tout, Tony Halstead, Anthony and Jill Saxton, Peter Cranham, Charles Weld, Dr Michael Pelly, Isabel Bass, Sir Harold and Lady Atcherley, George Benady, Heather Holden Brown, Penny Vincenzi, Neville Eldridge, Robbie Anderson, Mary Harboe, Mary Conisbee, Martin Gates, Terence Larkin, Professor Bruce Sayers, Alasdair Steven, David Warner, Derek Maynard and John Rendall.

SILVER WOLF

SILVER WOLF

TABLE OF CONTENTS

SILVER WOLF

Welcome to the world of *Silver Wolf*, the book that can help you change your life. I call the book *Silver Wolf*, because the silver wolf is the alpha male, its hair tinged with silver, and confident of its powers.

In this world, you are the alpha male, still young and strong, but now mature with the experience and knowledge of decades of life.

Silver Wolf is for the man in his fifties, who is ready to make a Grand Plan for years of happiness that no previous generation was ever privileged to enjoy.

It is about the time when you get your Third Act together, dust down your old dreams and ambitions, sort out your future finances, and take charge of your life.

Are you ready for it? It all depends on when that moment comes to you. That moment when you wake up one morning and ask yourself, *'What's it all about? What have I achieved? What am I going to do with the rest of my life?'* Psychologists often call this the male menopause; sociologists call it the eternal cry of middle-aged man.

Whatever you call it, you know when you've got it. And, when you've got it, you are ready to become a Silver Wolf. When you begin to wonder what you are going to do with the rest of your life, this is your guide. When you are ready to plan your new life, start turning these pages.

The belief of *Silver Wolf* is that the future should bring you the best years of your life. This is the time when you shake off the past, and plan to achieve those ambitions that fell by the way, while you were working hard 40–50 hours a week to pay the mortgage.

And this is the time when you fulfil those dreams that somehow you were never able to fit in to your working schedule.

If that is what you want for the next 20 years, then I wrote this book for you.

You are not ready for that strange existence that our parents called Retirement. I saw my parents' retirement and realised how it rarely worked. They both had busy jobs, in touch each day with dozens of people; then one Friday it was all over. Come Monday the phone was quiet, no one needed a decision from them, and it was as if they ceased to exist.

They moved from the family house, as millions did, to the small seaside flat, and so also lost touch with their old friends. For a few months they enjoyed their freedom, they visited every National Trust building in the county, and took long walks.

Then they both started to feel they had no function in life any more. Others of their age that they met on the promenade were also disappointed that the dreams of retirement had faded so quickly.

They were never really happy again, and I realised that their story was typical of millions. Retirement doesn't work. The idea of doing nothing for a couple of years might bring happiness to some, but doing nothing for another 20 years is obvious nonsense.

Retirement for you is no longer even an option. For you, there is a Third Act, when you create a new balance to your life of part work, part learning and part play. You make a new future and become part of a revolution in the pattern of life, as momentous as that of the Sixties.

You couldn't have arrived at this moment at a better time, if only for two reasons. You enter your Third Act as Ageism stumbles through its last dying days. Age Discrimination finally became as unlawful as Racism and Sexism in October 2006, and no longer can anyone be prevented from working, simply because they had passed some arbitrary age barrier.

In *Silver Wolf* I argue that some work should continue to be part of your newly balanced Third Act. That was often impossible for the previous generation, but for you the world has changed. Since April 2006 you could carry on working for the same employer while drawing an occupational pension.

From October 2006 there can be no discrimination by age in employment and, just as important, in vocational training.

The legislation in the autumn of 2006 confirmed the inevitable, and necessary, change in the whole ethos of corporate life. Companies, already aware that they needed your knowledge and experience, are now prepared for you gradually to cut down your days. That way they retain your contribution, while you can continue to work, but freeing more days for other parts of your new life.

Secondly, you reach your Third Act at a time when you should enjoy a longer and healthier Third Act than any generation of the past. Age expectancy is increasing by two years every decade, so that your expected life span is no longer three score and ten, but four score.

Far more important, these should be good years. Medical scientists have made phenomenal improvements in the control of ill health, and their knowledge doubles every three years.

On top of that, we have individually learnt that, if we look after our bodies, then they will look after us, without demanding too much attention.

With such a long and healthy life, and a changed working environment ahead, there can no longer be any thought of withdrawing from life, but only of plans to achieve what you most want to do in these decades.

To make these the best years of your life, you have, I suggest, only two things to do. The first is to rid yourself of any final hangovers about age that you may have inherited.

You now know that most of your parents' beliefs about ageing have turned out to be myths. Your mind will not inevitably decay, nor your body collapse. You are, in fact, more, not less, capable of learning, working and creating as you get older.

Based on that knowledge, your second task is to prepare for your Third Act. This is absolutely fundamental to your future happiness, whatever you decide to do, and the best way is to start today on your Grand Plan.

In order to create the right Grand Plan for you, you will want to ask yourself a lot of questions before you can begin planning.

These are questions that only you can answer; they lead to alternative scenarios which only you can decide; and include suggestions, the relevance of which to your future only you will know.

I have tried to cover most of the questions that will help you decide on your plan. What are your most important ambitions? What work will you do? Where will you live? What financial plans do you need to make? Do you want to make any changes in your character, appearance, or life style? Are you tempted to become a SKIer? What new skills do you want to learn? What old dreams do you now wish to fulfil?

These and other chapters are all aimed at helping you to be clear about the things you want to achieve in your Third Act. Only you can create your Grand Plan, which will be unique to you, and only you can make it happen.

Get your priorities right, get your balance of life right, and you will have mapped out your ideal way of life for your next 20 years.

By taking control of your life and following your blueprint for the future, you will enjoy years of fulfilment never possible to previous generations. They should also be years of great happiness, which is just about the most important thing all of us seek. The purpose of *Silver Wolf* is to help you find it.

PETER CARVELL   MAY 2006

NOTE: When I started *Silver Wolf* it was as a guide to men in their fifties. Then, as I talked with more people, I came to realise that that was too narrow an age group and many men in their very late forties and early sixties also found the book useful for them.

Then, after the first review copies, many have asked if it is also a book for women. The answer, of course, is Yes. I wrote it for men, as I didn't think I understood women well enough to cover their viewpoints, but, as it turned out, most of the chapters clearly apply to anyone of any sex, who is ready to create their Third Act.

I would be particularly proud if it also helps thousands of women to create a wonderful Third Act.

SILVER WOLF

- *Silver Wolf* is about your Third Act when you can finally achieve your dreams

- *Silver Wolf* is about making your Grand Plan for the two decades from your fifties onwards

- *Silver Wolf* is about doing what you always wanted to do, but never had time

- *Silver Wolf* is about being honest with yourself

- *Silver Wolf* is about dismissing the myths of ageism

- *Silver Wolf* is about keeping your mind alive and body fit

- *Silver Wolf* is about working to live, *not* living to work

- *Silver Wolf* is about a better sex life

- *Silver Wolf* is about *not* retiring from life

- *Silver Wolf* is about being proud of who you are

- *Silver Wolf* is about enjoying, and managing your money

- *Silver Wolf* is about Spending the Kids' Inheritance

- *Silver Wolf* is about raising new money

- *Silver Wolf* is about joining the most powerful voting lobby

- *Silver Wolf* is about being happy

CHAPTER 1

"I greatly enjoy the second blooming. Suddenly you find – at the age of 50, say – that a whole new life has opened before you."

Agatha Christie

Welcome to Your Third Act

Time to plan a new life and fulfil your dreams

Welcome to your Third Act. *Silver Wolf* is a book that can change your life. I say 'can' not 'will', because the decision to change is up to you. Make it and you will enjoy the happiest years of your life.

It is a guide to your third life, which I call the Third Act. Very few people in the history of the world have enjoyed a Third Act in their life, but you can, and it could be your best years.

This is the Act, which you begin usually in your fifties and carry forward into your seventies, when you plan, over these 20 or so years, to fulfil your hopes and dreams. For the first time you take control of your life, and you create the balance of activities that you want for the next two decades.

In your Third Act you make a new set of priorities for your future. You continue to work, as you did in your Second Act, but only for part of the time. You learn, as you did in your First Act, but again only part of the time. But, central to these, you make time for the pleasures that you always wanted to enjoy, and for the ambitions that you never found time to achieve in the previous 30 years.

Four things have combined to make your Third Act possible. The first is that we are living longer. The average life expectancy since you were born has gone up a couple of years with every decade. The Biblical three score and ten has now moved to four score. At 55 you can expect to live at least another 20 years, at 65 another 15.

The second is that advances in medicine will enable you to have not only a longer life, but a healthier one. You can expect to have no more illness in your sixties than you did in your forties; and you will probably be fitter than you were in the long days of endless working.

The third is that those financial pressures of paying off the mortgage and settling the children's education are usually over at some time in your fifties. The enormous sums that were eaten up by those investments can now be diverted to fulfilling some of your dreams.

The final change is in the number of years you are expected to work. The false phenomena of ageism has meant that millions over the last decades have been culled from the workplace, while still in their fifties. This has been disastrous for companies, who lost their most experienced people: and expensive for the country, as the cost of subsidising early retirement runs into some £30 billions a year.

But, it has also brought about a change in your life pattern. If society only wants a 35-year full-time working life from you, then this opens up a third life, a Third Act, when you can make a new life, with new aims, and a new balance.

Your parents rarely had this option. For them, that Second Act of working was longer, always over 40 years, and sometimes even 50 years. After this, they retired exhausted, hoping to enjoy a few years of what they called Retirement, a time for relaxing before moving on.

For you, retirement, in your parents' understanding of that word, is not even an option, and the old traditional patterns of the later part of our lives are now obsolete. Unlike your parents, you have a Third Act *before* you even think of retirement.

Whereas they had two Acts and an Epilogue, you have three full Acts, before any form of retirement. This is the dramatic change of today. You have a third chance at life, a Third Act longer than your First Act, a time to do whatever you decide.

The question is no longer how you can see out your years in an existence of non-work for which you have no qualifications.

The new question is what are you going to do with the next 20-year Act in your life, when you will be at your peak?

My answer is that you map out a Grand Plan for these years, laying out what it is you want to do. Look at yourself as you would a business, and make a serious plan of what you want to achieve, and how you will achieve it.

Establish in your own mind the priorities of your dreams and ambitions, and the balance that you wish to set between play, work, and learning. Go through your finances, so that you know if you have enough money for all your dreams, and whether you need to plan for more.

I have given it the grandiose title of Grand Plan, because that is what it is. It is your blueprint for this extraordinary third life that you can have. It is an extra reason why you can look forward to the next 20 years; it is the plan to do and be and achieve all those things that got lost in the rush of your Second Act.

Fortunately, there has never been a better moment for anyone moving through their fifties and about to create their Third Act. With Ageism becoming illegal from October 2006, companies will have to change their attitudes to the employment of older workers. Flexi-working and part time working are already normal for over a quarter of the working population, and cutting back the number of days that you work is no longer such a challenge.

Government, realising that it can no longer afford to subsidise those forced into leaving work early, is now reviewing the rules on pensions and allowances to encourage later part-time working.

Both parties realise that the bad old days of the Eighties and Nineties cannot go on. The great culling of the fifty plusses in those decades was a disaster for everyone concerned. Those days are over.

The Ageism Act may now make age discrimination illegal, but the changing attitude to age began before then, as the world began to understand that most myths about age were precisely that – myths. As you approach the creation of your Grand Plan, it is vital to remove any thoughts that getting older is an automatic handicap. You are just as capable now as you ever were, and probably even more so. So lose any parts of the debris of the old thinking that may have infiltrated your thinking.

We now know that Old has no meaning. At no age do you suddenly become old. Nothing dramatic changes in your mind or body at some particular age, whether that be 50, 60, or 70. You are as young or old as you look, behave and contribute.

You should, therefore, have no fear of ageing. You will not inevitably become senile, you will not lose your memory, and you will not lose the ability to learn at any age.

Your body will not collapse. It will get weaker each year from around 50, but, with more time for exercise, you will probably be fitter than you were at 40. Nor need you expect to be ill; most people have no more illness in their Third Act than they did in their Second.

Your parents were probably given a different story. They were told that decline was inevitable, that by 65 they were too old to work, that they could never be retrained, that they were probably going to be ill, and it was best if they just retired somewhere out of the mainstream of life. This attitude conveniently ignored that many of the greatest artists, composers, and scientists throughout history had done some of their best work after 60.

Fortunately that old-fashioned attitude is dying, which is why I believe that you are starting your Third Act at the best time ever. For you there is no drifting for years in a limbo of unemployment and aimlessness, as so many did before you.

For you, your Grand Plan will produce the glorious years of your Third Act, years when you define your place in the sun, strengthen your legacy, and become truly happy.

QUESTIONS

1. Are you personally ready to make a new life pattern for your Third Act?

2. How do you envisage your next 20 years, when work becomes only part of your life?

3. What do you most want to achieve?

CHAPTER 2

"Beautiful young people are accidents of nature, but beautiful older people are works of art."
Eleanor Roosevelt

Life is No Longer a Rehearsal

This is your Third Act; now you're on

The one simple purpose of this book is to remind you that, from your Fifties onwards, you now have another chance to achieve whatever you wanted in life.

Many of us may not have achieved it in our First Act, while we were learning, but we can blame that on our parents.

We may not have achieved all what we meant to do in our Second Act, when we worked flat out for 30–40 years, but we can blame that on the pressures to pay the mortgage, bring up the children, and have some savings.

This pressure, for many, took us along a path that was influenced by the need to earn more and more money, even when that career path took us away from where we really wanted to be.

Now, when we enter our Third Act, we have no one to blame if we don't achieve the fulfilment that we seek.

To enjoy these years, you can blend all parts of your life – work, play, creation, and learning – into a personal Grand Plan for happiness. There is no single formula for this Grand Plan, because we each have different priorities, start from different points, and aim to end up with different achievements.

Your Grand Plan is the sum of what you want to do to achieve your aims, feel fulfilled and be happy. The Plan will also be clear as to how you will achieve those aims; and the time frame for each part of the project. Your Grand Plan may not be set in stone, but it better be as right as you can make it – it's a 20-year plan to make your Third Act the best years of your life.

Before going into the personal questions that you may want to answer to make your own Grand Plan, there are 10 general points that I suggest are worth remembering.

1. Life is no longer a rehearsal. This is it

No more '*If only*', or '*One day I will*', or '*I always wanted to but.*' Your Third Act is when you're on. You've had a couple of rehearsals in the first two acts. This one is the big Third Act. This is when the hero wins out. Get your mind round that, and the rest follows.

2. Never think that the best years have gone. The best are about to begin

Some people had such good years at school or bringing up a family, or building up a business, that they may think they have had their best years. But, even for them, there can be better years ahead.

We all have decades of knowledge; we have the experience; you can now use that to make the next decades your best years. Only one thing can stop you, and that is your attitude. Get that right, and tomorrow, as the Americans insist on saying, starts the best days of your life.

3. Don't ever retire from life

By all means retire from your old job if it gives you no satisfaction, but don't retire from life and leave the world, unless you become a working monk.

Retirement was a bad idea, born in the 20th century, and it should have stayed there. We bipeds are essentially social beings, doers, hunters, learners, dreamers, and we flourish in the world, not out of it.

Retirement as a word should be banned from your thoughts. You are moving on, changing directions, playing on a new stage, starting this new life – anything except retiring.

4. Don't ever give up work

Work is a fundamental part of our lives, our self-esteem, our social standing. It is our counterbalance to leisure. Without some work, leisure becomes work. Work brings more money, longer life, and more enjoyable leisure. If you don't need to work for money, then work for free.

5. Don't ever be frightened about getting older

Nothing dramatically different happens to our bodies as we reach so-called significant ages. Sometimes your body goes wrong and needs repair, but you won't necessarily need more repairing in your sixties than you did in your forties. A small percentage of us will be unlucky, but five out of six of us enjoy a life no less healthy than before.

Don't ever think that the best times were when we were young. They were often the least satisfying years, and, for most people, life after 50 is far more satisfying.

Nor does your mind collapse. Evidence suggests that it does slowly decline after 50, but that only means that, by 70, your mental power is back to where it was at 30, when you thought it was at its peak!

6. Treasure your family and friends. Without love you grow old fast

Your inner circle is more important now than ever before. You need a support system for yourself, just as you become part of support systems for others. Now is the time to make new friendships, cherish old friends, settle any problems within the family. The Third Act is no time for petty differences; you have far more important things to do. Your home, family and friends are at the heart of your Grand Plan.

7. Be proud of your age

Too many people are quick to apologise for being older. Don't join them. Be proud of joining the most powerful group in the country. We've nothing to apologise for, and everything to give to those less fortunate than us.

We have experience and knowledge from 30–40 years of working. We have enough votes to control the next election. We own 80% of the wealth of the country. We are major players in the consumer market. We are, probably, wiser, more tolerant, nicer and better people than we have ever been.

8. Be optimistic. Smile and be happy

Trite? No, it is so important that maybe it should have come first. Smiling is important for three reasons. One, unless you're lucky, your mouth often looks miserable in repose. So smile. Two, people who are depressed are five times more likely to have a stroke. Not funny, so stay happy. Three, if you want to achieve the Great Plan, you need to be optimistic, so smile *and* be happy. Have fun. Remember fun? Well, it's time to bring it back.

9. Look after yourself

If you want to have a long, enjoyable and healthy life, then look after yourself. Your mind won't get slow from age, but it will from lack of use. Start it ticking over every day with a breakfast crossword, and keep it alive with new learning and new projects.

Of course, you will have 'senior moments', but they're no different from the 'middle-age moments' 20 years ago. Your brain still has 97% of your cells in use, and many people do their best work after 60.

Your body needs more help, because, if there's one of the clichés about getting old that is true, it is that our bodies get weaker every year. From around 50 we lose some 2% of our strength each year, which is why we have to give up some sports as we get older.

One of the best ways to keep fit is sex. Do it for fun, but also for your life. According to the BMA, sexually active men are far healthier and live longer.

10. Be honest with yourself

If you really are going to make these years the most fulfilling of you life, you can't fudge them. This is the time when you have a chance to decide what you really want to do, what legacy you want to leave, and how you can achieve happiness. Know yourself, don't lie to yourself. Be what you want to be; do what you want to do. This act is no rehearsal: this is it.

QUESTIONS

1. Which of these 10 points most surprises you?

2. Which change will you be happiest making?

3. Were you worried before about getting older?

CHAPTER 3

"Growing old is only a bad habit that a busy person has no time for."

Andre Maurois

For Your Eyes Only

The most important document for your next 20 years needs some answers from you first

Some of you may know exactly what you want to do with the next twenty years of your life. You may have been waiting years for a chance to achieve your dreams, and you may have all your priorities and timing clear.

If that is the case, you may not need this chapter. For everyone else, here are suggestions for approaching the creation of the most important Grand Plan in your life.

To make the transition from your years of full-time working to the creation of a new more balanced life needs a clear statement of where you are now, and what changes you intend to make to your life.

The Grand Plan for your Third Act is obviously all about your future, but I suggest, before you start on the plan, that you look into your past to do three exercises.

Why? Because only through seeing what you have done, and not done, can you really focus on what you want to do. In terms of the Grand Plan, this means looking at your strengths and being honest about what you missed. Remember, this is for a time in your life when *you* set the rules.

These three private documents are a simple way of your summing up your past and your present, before you embark on your new plans for the future. They are for your eyes only, so there is no point in dressing the truth, or being vague.

1. Describe yourself and your life until now, in no more than 500 words

This is a particularly useful exercise, because it reveals just how you see yourself. It should sum up your school days, your working days, your personal life and your relationships at the end of your Second Act and before the beginning of your Third.

This exercise sounds straightforward, but many people find that their first attempt is so unreal that they have to start again. This is *not* your CV. This is your summary of the key moments of your 50 plus years, and should include:

- what sort of person you have become
- how you think people see you
- what you bring to those around you
- what events changed your life
- what successes you are proudest of
- what you regret *not* having done
- what skills you have acquired
- what you own
- what relationships were important
- and so on...

You may find it easier to write this in the third person, if you are not used to writing about yourself. You may also find it easier at first, to dictate it into a recorder, before you input it onto the screen.

Whichever way you choose, don't make it too long, just a couple of pieces of paper, again for your eyes only – unless you really want to show it to someone else – and it is not a selling document.

It is a reminder for you of how you sum up your first two Acts. This can be a joyous or a painful experience, but, if you're honest in what you write, it should clarify the way ahead.

2. List your ten most important achievements so far

Your answers could be a mix of family moments, work

successes, sporting achievement, creative skills, or even personal battles that you have won.

Interestingly, in this exercise few answers are usually about work, but those that came out at recent seminars included a fair cross section:

- *Bringing up a good family*
- *Getting golf handicap down under 10*
- *Giving up smoking*
- *Changing homes at the right time*
- *Getting a 2:1 at university*
- *Becoming Head of House*
- *Marrying the right woman*
- *Marrying the right woman (finally)!*
- *Selling my first water-colour*
- *Founding a new charity*
- *Chairing the creation of the company's Five Year Plan*
- *Winning Salesman of the Year Award*
- *Winning the Club's tennis doubles three years in a row*
- *Still playing guitar in a Pop group at 52*
- *Surviving a difficult divorce*
- *Still able to run half marathon*
- *Getting my first book published at 50*
- *And so on…*

Your list is important, because it reveals to you what you regard as an achievement, and how many you have. Maybe you can think of over 30 important achievements, or maybe you have difficulty in finding 10. Either way, nearly everyone who does this exercise changes over half the list before they think they've reached their true one.

3. List 10 important things that you think you want to add during your Third Act

This is nothing more than an indulgence at this stage, but

worth doing now, before you start the serious thinking. You may have quite different answers, but recent seminars included these:

- *Fly over the Grand Canyon*
- *Learn to play the violin*
- *Work less*
- *Speak Italian fluently*
- *Re-landscape the garden*
- *Spend more time helping the children*
- *Write my autobiography*
- *Become less dogmatic*
- *Write a novel*
- *Build a B2L portfolio*
- *Set up my own consultancy*
- *Buy a vineyard and have my own chateau name*
- *Learn to control my temper*
- *Spend more time with my wife*
- *Spend time in the sun*
- *Never wear a tie again*
- *Finish the Times crossword each morning, not just on Saturday*
- *Personally build an extension on the house*
- *Study for a degree in modern history*
- *Ride across Arizona*
- *Start a disco club for 40 plusses*
- *Do some work in a Third World country*
- *Take over our investment portfolio*
- *And so on…*

These three exercises are the starting point, the encapsulation of your past up to your present. Once you've done these honestly, with no self-deception, you should expect to have a clear outline, at least in your mind, of where your life is now, what you have achieved in the first 50 plus years, and perhaps some of the gaps that you may now wish to fill.

Now, I suggest, you need to ask yourself a series of questions, before you begin on your Grand Plan. These are easy questions to ask, but, for most of us, difficult to answer. Many are questions that we meant to answer years ago, but never made the time; some are questions we never wanted to answer because there didn't seem any point then.

There is every point now. To make your Third Act the time when you fulfil your dreams and ambitions, you need to answer them truthfully, because your answers will be the basis for your Grand Plan.

There are dozens of questions that are useful in making your next decades the best yet, but I suggest you start with these 10. Some are about your dreams, some about your relationships, and some practical about your work and your finances.

What these ten questions have in common is that they can only be answered by you. As before, there is little point in answering them untruthfully or vaguely. They are about your life and happiness, and merit a straight answer.

10 Questions to Answer before You Create Your Grand Plan

1. **What do you really want for yourself in the next 20 years?**
   This is about you and you alone. What will give you happiness? The wish to be happy is probably the one thing common to all of us, but do you know what would make you happy?

   If you woke up tomorrow, and a voice said to you that all your dreams had come true, what would you see? What do you hear? What can you smell? Where would you be, who would be with you? What would you be learning that day? What work is part of your life?

2. **Are you happy with your family and friends?**
   Are you and your partner happy to go on for another 20

years? Are there any family conflicts that need solving? Are your children a key part of your life? Is your life filled with enough love? Do you have enough good friends?

3. **Where do you want to live?**
   Do you want to stay in the same home? In the same area? Does your home work for you, in the way it is laid out and used? Do you want a second home? Do you want to spend time in the sun? Would you prefer to live alone, or with others? Do you want to live near your children and parents, or worlds away?

4. **How much work do you want to do?**
   Do you need to work for money, or do you just want to work as part of your new balanced life? How many days a week? Do you want to start your own company? What work would you most prefer to do?

5. **What do you want to learn?**
   Do you want to study for a degree? Develop your creative abilities, write a book, paint, or make music? Do you need to learn a new trade for a new career, or develop skills that you previously had no time to pursue?

6. **What pleasures do you want to enjoy?**
   A home in the sun? A silver convertible? The latest technological toys? Travelling the world? Playing the great golf courses? Being the heart of a three-generation family? Three-day weekends doing nothing? Finding a satisfying credo?

7. **Do you have enough money or do you need to reorganise your finances?**
   Do you have enough funds to finance your dreams? Will your money survive inflation? Can it be invested more efficiently? Do you know your exact financial situation? Do you need to change your budget or your dreams? What does your money give you?

8. **What values do you hold, and what spiritual beliefs are important to you?**
   Do you believe in a God? What moral code guides you? Are there clear rules by which you lead your life? Do you want to be less materialistic? Do you have spiritual goals?

9. **Are there things you want to change to be a better person?**
   What don't you like about yourself? Are there any major faults you want to remove? Are you a giver or a taker in personal relationships? Do you want to change the way you behave in any way? Are there personal qualities, which you believe you lack, but could now achieve? Do you want to change your appearance?

10. **Are you ready to remake your life?**
    Do you have the abilities to take control of your life? Do you need to change any part of your present lifestyle? Do you want your life continuing in its present pattern, or are you ready to change everything?

You are now going to live a life dedicated to what is important to you. That is why you need to answer questions, about yourself and your dreams, that you haven't dared ask for many years. Later chapters go into many of these subjects in more details, but, based on your answers to yourself, you can now begin to create your Grand Plan.

QUESTIONS

1. Which of the three documents did you find the most difficult?

2. Out of the 10 questions, which was the easiest for you to answer?

3. Are you now clearer as to what you want to achieve in your Third Act?

CHAPTER 4

"What you're 'retiring' to is ten times more important than what you're retiring from."
Lin Schreiber

The Making of Your Grand Plan
It will take time, but it will change your life

Once you've answered the questions in the previous chapter to your satisfaction, you are ready to start on the actual making of your Grand Plan. It is not something you can do quickly, and it is too important to you to rush. This, after all, is the blueprint for your next 20 years.

From my own experience, and that of many friends now in their early 60s, I have to tell you that it can easily take six months, not to do a first outline, which is comparatively easy, but before you are convinced that you have got it all right.

The reason for the Grand Plan is to so organise your life that you fulfil many of your dreams, and achieve some of your ambitions. This is the time to be totally honest with what you want to be and do. This is a serious presentation to a serious client: You. You are the client now and you are making this presentation to yourself.

What your dreams are, only you know. They are often a mixture of things to be learnt, places to be seen, business projects to be achieved, relationships to be improved, all wrapped up in a quality of life that was impossible in your Second Act.

Your Third Act is a dramatic time in your life. You are about to create a new balance between your work and your personal fulfilment. You are about to balance your budget, not to pay the mortgage, but to finance the achieving of your personal dreams.

It is the most enormous challenge, but get this change right, and your whole life will receive a surge of energy that should send it into an existence that seemed impossible only a year ago.

To achieve this you need to create your own Grand Plan, and it will include at least the following stages.

The Six Steps to Your Grand Plan

- **Set out your dreams**
- **Calculate your finances**
- **Organise your work plans**
- **Prepare a first draft of the Grand Plan**
- **Discuss it with your partner**
- **Finalise the Grand Plan**

1. Set out your dreams for the Third Act

This is the enjoyable start; this is the time of goose-girling. The first challenge is getting clear precisely what dreams are just vague wishes, and which are the ones that you really want to do. Then comes the task of putting them into some kind of priority, so that, if some have to be sacrificed, then you know which they are.

A dream does not have to be of world-shattering importance; it is something, which you wish to do and now intend to make time to do it. As I wrote this, I was thinking of what various friends and acquaintances have done.

I have some who always wanted to challenge their bodies and have become a variation of Action Man. Two have climbed Kilimanjaro (not difficult, but forbidden to anyone over 68; now there's ageism for you); another spends his holidays scuba-diving through ancient temples in the Mediterranean.

Perhaps it's because flying gives you a symbolic sense of freedom, but half of them seem to have obtained pilot's flying licences in either Florida or Portugal.

Several are doing things in property. Four have bought second homes in the sun; one had always wanted to convert an old building into his dream home, and is doing that somewhere in Burgundy. Another is developing his old home in Wiltshire by building a separate house at the end of the garden.

Others wanted to paint, write, or make music, and are now trying to do these. Some are writing their first novel; others are writing their autobiographies. One friend is even writing a musical based on the 'Gunfight at the OK Coral', which he apparently has dreamt of doing for years.

Yamaha keyboards have appeared in most houses, and one friend even has a small studio, which he is using as a business to give young musicians, pop and classical, a chance to record.

Tools in the garden sheds have had to give way to easels in some families. Watercolours seem to be more popular than oils, but I do have one ex-colleague who seems to be inspired more by Jackson Pollock than Russell Flint.

Everyone seems to be feverishly learning Spanish or Italian, and brushing up on their schoolboy French. Gone are the Mozart or Sinatra CDs from the car, to be replaced with language lessons. Two are studying for degrees; three for Diplomas in something.

Still others have used their non-workdays to work for causes they believe in. One of them is now helping the Red Cross in Russia, another giving a day a week to help set up better web sites for non-profit organisations.

Only one has gone into local politics, another is aiming for a PhD in Business Psychology. The most esoteric dream being fulfilled is by a man who has long wanted to track the paintings of Louis Brea for a monograph on the artist. I am full of admiration, but secretly wonder if he would take so long if the paintings weren't mainly along the French Riviera.

Travel does seem to be a major part in many Grand Plans. Following in the footsteps of the 19th century Grand Tourists figures large, and one friend is going as far as producing a Diary of the Grand Tour, together with photographs, taken with his new Minolta digital SLR. I know of no one going round the world, but several who have visited Dubai, Las Vegas, Cape Town, Singapore, and Shanghai.

Most of their dreams seem to be modest, and all of them fit

their personal pilgrimages into a new, balanced life. The point is to set your own 'dream'. This book is a guide to fulfilling it.

2. Cost your new life

It's fun having dreams, setting out things you want to do, places you want to visit, excitement you want to enjoy, disciplines you want to learn. The boring part is costing them, but it is necessary for the obvious reason – they all cost money, and that money has to be possible within your own financial situation.

Money isn't the most important part of your Third Act years, but lack of it is. Your Grand Plan must make financial sense, if you don't want to have to worry. The budgets for fulfilling any of your dreams should be laid out at least for the first ten years, and you will want to be certain that each year's proposed cash flow can be covered.

The only way you can be certain about this is by doing a total review of your financial situation. Even those, who have done family budgets before, can find this daunting. It's easiest to do it on your computer with the Excel Spreadsheet, or equivalent.

At this stage you are only preparing a rough outline, but whichever way you do this first financial draft, for most us it shows only one thing – you have less money than you need, and far less than you want!

'*Don't panic*', as Corporal Jones used to shout. Even in this simplistic form, you now know the worst. You know roughly how much you need to earn now, and how much you need from fees and investments five, ten years down the line. *(See Chapter 7)*

3. Organise your working life

The next step is to organise your working days. The Third Act is based on the premise that you do not stop work completely, and that it is an important part of these years. This is the time when you allocate work to being a part of your life, not the whole that it has been. Your Third Act is about combining less work with more achievement of your dreams.

There are probably three main alternatives. You may wish to stay with your existing company but work less; to move to a company that welcomes your skills on a part-time basis; or to set yourself up in your own consultancy, selling your time to a number of clients.

In an ideal world, you may decide to reduce the number of days you work gradually, from five to four to three and so on, depending on how much you enjoy your work, and how much income you want to earn.

The most relaxed way to do this is to stay with your existing company, where they know your worth, you know the clients, and you can help to bring on others, without being any competition to them. You can do this as a contracted, self-employed person, costing the company no national insurance or pension contributions.

If you want to take your independence further and have a service that could be used by several companies, then set up your own consultancy. This is not a complicated procedure. Create a name under which you will trade, apply to be VAT registered if that helps you, print some stationary, and you're in business.

One cautionary note: I have several friends who set up their own consultancies, but being a sole trader is not easy, and those who fared best all took the consultancy route with partners.

What is important is that you move towards a time when you continue to enjoy the social and financial benefits of work, but it is only part of your life. This may take some time and planning, and that is another reason why your planning of the great leap into the Third Act can take longer than you imagined. *(See Chapter 8)*

4. Prepare the first draft of your Grand Plan

As soon as you have clarified what it is that you want to do in your Third Act, and what the financial situation is, then prepare a first proposal for your Grand Plan. This should be done in the same way as you have presented proposals in the past to clients and colleagues.

It should show what it is that you want to do, and the reasons for it. It should show a suggested timetable, and explain why the timing makes sense. It should show the cost of these proposals and the total outlay, once they are added to the normal family budget.

It should then lay out the revenue expected, and show the contribution from each source, together with any explanations for these figures. A further section should outline all future income that might be expected from investments, and any relevant timing of each item.

Make a Summary from all these, then make up two copies of your draft Grand Plan in yellow folders, with the word DRAFT on the cover. Yellow because it is a draft; your revised version will need a red folder. When the plan is finally agreed, it can go into your blue folder.

I only introduce a note of formality to stress the importance of this document. It is the blueprint for your life. How quickly your Grand Plan can go into a blue folder depends not only on you, but on your partner.

5. Discuss your dreams with your partner

You now need to show your partner your Grand Plan. I have to tell you that this could be the most difficult moment of your life. At best, expect understanding; at worst, the mother of all scenes.

Suddenly, you present your partner with a plan that may be far from the life she was expecting as you got older. She may not begin to see why you want to start this gradual rebalancing of your work and dreams.

Apart from that, she may have her own agenda, which is very different from yours, and be horrified to find she does not begin to understand you. She knew that life was going to be different once the children had left the nest. She knew that the two of you were going to have to find a new way of living together, but now you are suddenly presenting her with a life plan that doesn't seem to include her.

I add that last warning, because I have one friend who received such a blast from his partner – and deserved it. His draft plan was cold and impersonal, it was full of what he would do and scarcely had a 'we' in it. Don't make the same mistake. The plan should have the efficiency of a business proposal, but the understanding that it is for the personal happiness of both of you.

It is true that this period of your life often requires a new, and sometimes, radical reappraisal of what you want and need from each other. This is the time for finding a new way of happiness together, or making a break, while both of you are still young.

Divorce is spreading like an epidemic for those in their 50s, but it need not, if you talk honestly and want to make the marriage work. It could, in fact, bring new life back into a relationship. Nothing is more bonding than undertaking some thing together. Stagnation is the killer of most relationships.

In fact, of a dozen friends who had discussions on their Grand Plan proposals, only two divorced, when they found they wanted totally opposite lives in these years, and also realised that there wasn't much love left to hold them together. Two others had dramatic and often bitter fights, before reconciliation; but eight had pleasant discussions and found an agreed programme within a month.

What is important for your happiness in your Third Act is that you and your partner are clear about what each want. One in five couples in their fifties today find there isn't enough love and respect left to make a new partnership with a different game plan, and they break up.

It is often a decision soon regretted, and usually it is through lack of sensible communication. It may need more honest talking than you have had between you for a long time, but it is worth every effort to make a new, happy life.

6. Prepare the final version of your Great Plan

In the light of your family discussions, your plan will certainly need some reworking, and it will be all the better for it. I know of many who changed it half a dozen times before it made sense, the objections faced, the work in place, the investments tweaked. What rarely change are the dreams to be fulfilled, because that is what your Third Act is ultimately about.

When you finally decide that the plan is true, agreed and do-able, put it into blue folders. It is now your blueprint for your new life.

QUESTIONS

1. Would you prefer to design the plan on your own, or work it through with your partner from the beginning?

2. Which part of the planning are you most looking forward to?

3. How long do you expect to take before your personal Grand Plan is ready?

CHAPTER 5

"Old age is like everything else. To make a success of it you have to start young."

Fred Astaire

When Do You Start Your Grand Plan?

Fifty something is ideal, but you will know when you are you ready

O f course, you can start your Third Act at any time between 45 and 65, but the ideal time is in your early fifties. You may think this is too early, you are still in full flight in your career, and couldn't possibly start thinking about a different kind of life. And that may be right for you, but I promise you that a number of things come together in the mid-fifties which make it the right time for most.

Here are 10 reasons why around 45 + VAT is often the right time.

- You are still young, even though you have now crept into the era that is called middle-aged. You are on the plateau of your powers, and can handle a new venture with confidence

- You can expect at least 20 good years ahead of you, before you might want to slow down

- You have probably finished paying for your home, or at least have little yet to pay. Very soon the mortgage will not be taking up a large chunk of your income, which may allow you to earn less, or divert the old mortgage money into some other project

- Your home is certainly worth a great deal more than you paid for it, and you have therefore good collateral for raising capital for a new venture, whether it be to start your own company, buy a second home, or further another of your dreams

- If you have children, they will probably shortly be leaving home. This raises questions about whether you now need such a large home or wish to move

- With the children going, you are now beginning a new relationship with your partner, and may be uncertain as to how this will work out

- Statistically you have reached the peak of your earnings. I don't mean you, but, in the last two decades, most people's earnings have increased until they are somewhere between 53 and 55, and then fall away

- If you are in a large company, it's around this time that they may ask you in for a cosy chat on how you see your future, and ask if 'early retirement' sounds attractive to you. With ageism illegal from October 2006, this habit will hopefully change, but it does give you a chance to discuss part-time working

- You have already worked over 30 years in the rat race, and may be ready for a change of direction

- Finally, you may well have the Fifties Blues. According to psychologists this is a classic time of discontentment for many of us, a time when we're likely to say something like:

  "I've worked hard for many years, trying to pay the mortgage, pay the children's school bills, give the family a decent life style, and what have I got out of it? Not much.

  "I never seem to have enough time to do anything except work. My wife and I have drifted apart; the children are leaving. I'm overweight, follicly-challenged, and unfit. And

what have I achieved? Not very much. What's the point of it all?"

This lament can go on for hours, the psychologists say, (or, if you listen to some people, years) and it's all very real. It's all part of the male menopause. In the past, this unhappiness dissolved relationships, and sent you into a long wait for retirement; today it can disappear as you make your Grand Plan.

Can the Third Act begin earlier? Of course it can, if you have the funds to make it possible to exist with less earnings. A decade ago, I knew many people who thought at the end of their forties that they had almost enough money to step off the daily ritual, reduce the amount of time they worked, and could start on realising their dreams.

They were clear what they wanted to do, and had made their plans long before reaching 55. What they didn't have was the confidence that their money would be enough for 30 years; nor that they would be able to work part time.

And, they were right. Ten years ago, part-time employees were rarely welcomed by companies; and most people's wealth was tied up in a house that had fallen in value, with a mortgage costing 12%.

Today everything is very different. More companies now realise the importance of keeping experienced staff and accept the need for part-time working. Your property has doubled in value; re-mortgaging is cheap when you need capital; and dramatic improvements in health are giving you not just a longer life, but a healthier life.

Even more often at seminars, people ask if 60 is too old to start. Again, of course it is not. Leaving it to your sixties has the obvious disadvantage of giving a shorter period of time before you may want to retire to some bucolic life, but equally your finances should be in much stronger shape.

I know many who are working full time into the sixties and then are beginning their Third Act by gradually cutting back the days they spend working, year by year.

When you personally start depends on you, your attitude and

your financial position. You need enough money to make the change viable, and, just as important, you need the mental approach that makes you ready to opt out of the old pattern and begin a new life. When they coincide, you are ready to begin.

Your fifties are a watershed in your life, whatever you decide to do and whatever life you decide to lead. This is the time when you take charge of your life and start a new period, which I have called your Third Act.

That is why I have proposed in earlier chapters that you create a Grand Plan for yourself, in which you make a new balance for your life, combining your work, your learning and your personal pleasures. But its success depends on you, and the changes in your life may also need to include changes in you.

The transition from letting the world run your life to your running it is enormous. You have now taken charge, and you have to have enough confidence in yourself to carry it through.

You may already have all the characteristics and virtues to handle this new plan. Check them against this list.

10 Attributes for Success in Your Third Act

1. **You need to be prepared**

   It's the old Boy Scout message, but it has never been more apposite. The more prepared you are, the more chance you have of making a success of your Third Act.

   Know what you are going to do; know how the money will be there to fund your new life; and know that your support team understand you – just as you will support them in their dreams.

   If you've never been a planner before, now is the time to start. This is not a seat of the pants operation; it is a long term Grand Plan.

2. **You need to clear away the debris from the past**

   Not just the excessive amount of things that seem to fill your home, but the hangovers from old hurts, misunderstand-ings, and mistakes that you and others may have made. Clear them all up. You cannot go forward into a new life with old scars.

The same approach applies to old habits and attitudes. We all adopt some that are not to our credit, but seemed useful in the old life. They are not needed now. Clear them all from your mind.

3. **You need to give yourself time**

For 30 years you were possibly always busy, or, at least, thought you were. It's easy to confuse busyness with useful productivity; perhaps you often hurried through life, rarely stopping, as the cliché has it, to smell the roses. That's a relic from the past.

In your Third Act you make time to relax. Time to listen to others. Time to enjoy being, not only doing.

This sometimes seems to be the hardest change for people to make. Often it takes a year before they come to realise that they can get more done in less time than ever before, and so have more time to enjoy life.

4. **You need to learn how to have fun again**

Make it part of your life to do some things just for fun. *'I'm too busy for that'* is one of the remarks that are now out of your vocabulary.

It isn't a sin to have fun. If you can't actually enjoy it at first, think of it as a therapy. To have fun, to smile, to laugh is good for your health. After a year you may be able just to enjoy it.

5. **You need to be courageous**

What you're about to do needs courage. You need the courage of your own convictions that this revolution in your life will bring wonderful benefits. You need the courage to throw out much of your past. You need the courage to admit any faults, and become the kind of person you always meant to be.

6. **You need to be persuasive**

   Nothing is ultimately more important to your success with the Grand Plan than the love and support of those around you. You need their help as never before, and you need to win them to your plans.

   This is the time to use all your skills in persuasion, but remember that understanding their viewpoints is more important than opposing them. After 30 years of making decisions at work, most of us have come to realise that we are only right three times out of five – if lucky.

7. **You need to manage your money**

   In your Grand Plan you will have spread out your financial position, but you now will want to manage it better than ever before, because you need it to cover a couple of decades. Inflation alone will mean that you will need twice as much money for the same quality of living by the end of that time.

   This means your keeping a financial controller's eye on all your costs and revenues for two main reasons: one, not to waste money, like having the wrong insurance policies; and two, more importantly, to avoid any unexpected panics. *(See Chapters 7 & 16)*

   Sufficient money does not guarantee a happy Third Act, but worry over money can certainly spoil your happiness.

8. **You need to stay optimistic**

   You need to believe in yourself more than ever. You are now in charge of your life, you have worked out what you want to do, and you must never doubt your ability.

   Be confident that what you do now is right for you. If you have moments of doubt, remind yourself of the list you wrote of your dreams. The glass is <u>always</u> half full.

9. **You need to stay young**

   Never think about age; it is never relevant. Never use age as an excuse for anything. Just remind yourself that the old stories were all myths. If you still have hang-ups about your age, this is the time to start lying. So take some years off your age; five is fine, and don't go further than ten.

Even if you don't need to lie to any future employers about your age, you may still want to lie to yourself. Sociologists have all kinds of clichés about age. You are as old as you look. You are as old as you feel (or, as Groucho Marx said, '*You are as old as the woman you feel*'). You are as old as you act.

But one cliché is, I suspect, true for many of us. We are as old as we tell ourselves we are. You may be too young at 53 to realise yet, but there are stereotypic behaviour patterns for different biological ages, and it is only too easy to slip into them. I recommend you stay 53 for years.

10. **You should feel proud of yourself**
You have so much to be proud of. The work you did for over 30 years. The family that you and your partner brought up. And now the creation of your new life. You have joined the ranks of those who have gone on in later years to produce a new legacy.

Creative people never stop. Many artists, writers, scientists, archaeologists, engineers, academic professors, and inventors have produced their best work in the last 25 years of their life.

You have joined those who never think of retiring to do nothing, but who know their worth and continue to contribute to life.

Your Third Act is not a game you play; it's for real. You no longer have to act the role that you may have adapted for your previous life. This is when you are totally honest with yourself about who you are, how you see your relationship with others, what you stand for, and what you want to achieve. With this honesty you will be able to achieve happiness, and that, after all, is the real purpose of the next two decades.

QUESTIONS

1. When do you expect to be ready to start your Grand Plan?

2. Do you need to change any of your attitudes?

3. Are you looking forward to creating your Third Act?

CHAPTER 6

"I don't want to spend the rest of my life bringing up a young and inexperienced house!"

Jerome K. Jerome

Where do You Want to Live?

At last it can be whatever and wherever you want

Before you get too far along the plan, I suggest that what you decide to do with your home is one of your key decisions.

Not only is it your base and the starting point for whatever you might want to do, but it is also a financial asset, which can serve your needs for the future. Your home is more important to you now than ever before, for three reasons.

First, you will now be spending more time in it. It becomes more than the place where you sleep in between 10-hour work days; it is now the HQ for your new life, and needs to supply the atmosphere, space and facilities that you need to achieve your ambitions.

Secondly, the value of your home has certainly more than doubled in the last few years. Your home has, therefore, become more than just your home – it is your main investment, and probably worth more than all your other investments put together.

Thirdly, you can now borrow against it more easily and more cheaply than any other generation.

You've paid off your mortgage – or at least most it – the children are off on their own, and, at some time, you have the luxury of not only deciding where and how you want your new home to be, but also how you will use this untapped capital.

The classic old advice was that, once the children had gone, and you no longer worked full time, then you should sell your home, and buy something smaller and cheaper. This may not be right for you, but it is a valid view for a number of reasons:

- You may prefer to take profits from a sale of the home now, because you can buy a smaller home for half the price, and it would be quite reassuring to have the odd hundred thousand more pounds to use

- You may welcome a smaller home and garden to look after, just in case something happens to your old Cresta Run wound, and you don't want such a large home to look after

- You may welcome the excuse to cut back on bedrooms so the family can't all descend on you

- You may want to start a new life in another town or move further into the countryside, with a less stressful life

- You may want the money to buy a second home in the sun, so that you can enjoy two different worlds

- You may want the money to invest in a Buy to Rent property

- You never liked the old home anyhow, and would like to start again and make a different home that fits your needs

Equally, there are good reasons for the opposite decision, and keeping your existing home:

- You may actually like your home. You've worked on it over the years, you've come to accept its deficiencies and enjoy its advantages. You would prefer to adapt the old home to meet the needs of your new life

- If you are continuing to work, albeit part-time, with the same company, then you may need to be in the same area

- If you are planning to set up your own consultancy from home, then you may need all the rooms you have

- If you are hoping to keep your local friends, and visit your local haunts, then you won't want to move

- If you want to enjoy the same standard of living as now, then there's no point in jobbing down to a couple of beds in a flat near the sea

- If you want family or friends to stay, there's no point in moving to a smaller home

- You'd prefer to raise any capital you need on your existing home, and save the moving costs

There are plenty of good reasons for either decision, and there is no right or wrong answer. As always with the making of your Grand Plan, only you can know what is best for your happiness. I am sure you will know friends who have already made their decisions, but here are three real-life cases from friends of mine, who took quite different decisions for quite different reasons with their homes. All are now five years into their Third Act.

The first, Robert, decided to downsize. The estate agents told him that most of their big sales now came from people selling the old family home and moving into something smaller. He wanted some extra cash, and so this made sense to him.

In his Grand Plan he was continuing to work part-time, so he needed to stay in the same area, but he felt that he needed extra money, more than he needed the extra rooms. He found that smaller homes were far more expensive than he had realised, but did eventually find what they wanted for about two-thirds of the money from the sale of the old home.

He lost two bedrooms on the change, and half the garden, but gained an annexe, where he could easily work. With the capital that he freed, he bought a flat in a Buy to Let scheme, for the simple reason that his financial plan had showed him one basic fact. Ten years down the road he would need a good deal of money to carry on.

He was disillusioned with shares, and decided that property

would be the answer for him. His argument was the classic one, that it is the gearing that makes the difference, and he was going to borrow 75% of the cost, and only put up 25% himself. The cost of the interest repayments and maintenance would, he hoped, be covered by rental income. *(See Chapter 17)*

Only time will tell, but right now he has a home he's happy with, and a business that should pay off in ten years time. He wishes they had a third bedroom, and says that that was a mistake, as they have to put up some of the family at the local hotel. But for them it was the right decision at the time, and the extra capital also makes possible more of the long weekends away that they both enjoy.

For Michael there was never any other decision; he had to stay in the family home. For him the children were the centre of his life, and he wanted bedrooms for all the generations, and a large garden where the grandchildren could play.

He decided to keep the old home, and make it exactly as he wanted for his Third Act. He added rooms on, so that he had his own den, and an extra guest room. All this was done round the old pool, which then became a heated indoor pool, much more used and adding £20,000 more in value to the house.

All that was not financially possible without re-mortgaging the house. He almost organised enough earnings from his new consultancy to cover the interest on a lifetime mortgage, and the children agreed that any sums of money, which he could legally give them each year, would, when necessary, go to pay off the mortgage.

His answer has worked for him so far. He still has the old home, he can still host the family, he has made the improvements that make the home better for him and his partner, and each improvement has increased the value of the property.

The lawyer and the accountant have changed the form of ownership to tenancy in common, and set up trusts to ameliorate the effect of CGT. When he does need more money, he intends to borrow heavily against the house with an equity release life mortgage, both to keep up the standard of living and reduce the CTT. *(See Chapter 15)*

For Robin, circumstances were different. He and his partner nearly broke up in the first three years of living alone after the children went. They finally fought through what is often the most traumatic part of the Third Act, and decided that the answer was to start again in a different world. They wanted to live in the sun, and that became central to their Grand Plan.

They nearly broke up again in arguments over whether it should be Spain, France or Italy, but in the end agreed that southern Spain had the most sun, and settled on a development in Estepona.

They kept their UK home, because they knew that they might one day want to return, and knew, equally, that they might not be able to afford to come back, if they had to start again.

They borrowed 70% of the cost of their Spanish home against their UK earnings, and put up the initial 30%, plus 10% costs, by remortgaging their UK house. The Grand Plan was for them to work like mad in the UK for three more years, before cutting back on their work, and moving down to Estepona for the winter months, as an experiment.

They finally did this, rented their UK home for six months, and moved to the sun for six winter months. In the Spring, they returned to England and rented out their Estepona home for the summer to pay the mortgage. And so currently they live in two homes, and rent out whichever one they are not using.

They are prepared to accept that this means strangers coming into their houses, and that they must close up after every six months, but this is acceptable to them, while they are deciding on their future life.

This also makes it possible for them to enjoy two homes and two very different lifestyles, without much extra cost. With both homes, the rental income covers the basic running costs, and they still can enjoy the capital growth on both properties.

In Spain they are busy learning the language, painting, writing, and helping out at a charity. When they speak Spanish fluently, they have a business that they plan to start in Spain.

Again, this has been the right decision for them so far. They feel they are fully in touch with family and friends on the web, they make use of the new VoIP telephone services to have free international phone calls, and they have a fairly basic, and totally unreliable, video-conferencing set-up to keep in touch with their work in the UK.

So far they are happy, and are following the Grand Plan to give them a new life, and a much happier time together.

Whatever you decide is best for you, your decision as to where and how you live is obviously based on more than just financial considerations. It's just as important to have a home that gives you pleasure and works for your new lifestyle.

You'll find you get a lot of advice from the old school on what you should do about your home in this period of you life. Much of it, I believe, is dubious. These are the old myths:

- *Best to go into a small home, so it's not too much to handle, as you get older.* Wrong attitude. By all means move to a smaller house, but not for this reason. If you can't handle a normal home, then go and get fit. Have a small home, if that's right for you, but it can be mentally and physically restricting, and not ideal for a full ongoing life.

- *Better a flat than a house.* Wrong. Stairs are natural fitness equipment; the more we go up and down the better. The statistical evidence is clear, that people in houses live fitter and longer lives than those in flats, simply because running up and down stairs has been called the perfect exercise for lazy people.

- *Move to the country, the air's better.* True, and it is another historical fact that country people live longer than those in towns. But it all depends on which country and which town. It is much easier to stagnate in the country, away from urban life, if it has little stimulus. Are you really a country person? It is not always the idyll which townies imagine. Totally a personal choice.

- *Paint your home in neutral colours.* Not if you find it depressing. Be bold. Your home in these years should reflect you in every way. You want red walls in the kitchen and dining room? Paint them. You want yellow ochre walls in the bedrooms? Paint them.

Your next home is for your new life; it should reflect you and your partner. It should have the spaces you need to carry out your Grand Plan; it should have the colours and styles that give you pleasure every time you arrive home. It is now your home, your headquarters, and your comfort zone.

It's not for the children; not for corporate entertaining; not for passing traffic. Turn whatever home you have into the place you always wanted to have.

All that I have tried to show is that, once you are clear as to the way you want to live, then don't forget to use the value in your home to make it all possible.

QUESTIONS

1. In your Grand Plan do you want to keep your family home or downsize?

2. If you sell, how will you use the new capital?

3. Will you want to have two homes?

CHAPTER 7

"It's not hard to meet expenses; they're everywhere."
Bob Hope

Do You have Enough Money?

The last thing you need in your Third Act is money worries, so do your sums now

Here is the serpent in the paradise of longevity. Living for at least another 20–25 years requires more money than most of us had planned. Just gentle inflation at 3% a year will double your financial needs before that period is over.

Your budgets for the Third Act need more attention to strategy, more honesty in estimation, and less dressing with optimism than any you may ever have done in the previous 30 years. You now have to organise your own finances in such a way that they can pay for the next 20 years.

This is a fascinating but terrifying exercise, because, probably for the first time, you have to factor in long-term inflation, changing plans, and likely income reduction. Whichever way you do the first draft, if you're like most of us, it shows only one thing – you have, as I wrote before, less money than you need, and far less than you want.

Those figures dotted across your computer's Excel spread sheet are your future. They are the rock on which your dreams will become real or founder. Where the figures don't make sense and clearly come short of what you need, then you have to plan a way by which you will be able to fund those dreams.

Most of the people I know found this exercise alternatively the most enjoyable and the most horrifying of all the preparations for their Grand Plan, but for all of them it was the one they got wrong the most.

Each time that they went over the figures again, they realised that they had forgotten something else, and had to redo them. The shock of seeing costs continue to rise and income often decreasing is a sobering thought.

This is why it is better to start this exercise early in your fifties, so that you still have plenty of time to plan future income streams, and reorganise your investments, after you have worked out the cost of achieving your dreams and ambitions. What you are doing, above all other considerations, is finding the answers to four basic questions.

1. **How much income do I have coming in for certain, in the next five, ten, fifteen years?**

2. **How much do I need, to match the total made by the family budgets, increased by inflation only, plus the projects that are in my Grand Plan?**

3. **If I need more than we can expect to receive, can I find all the extra money from working, or will it need to come partly from other sources? If so, what sources?**

4. **What investments and savings do I have for the future? Will they cover all future long-term liabilities, or will I need to raise loans?**

You will have your own way of preparing budgets, but here are some obvious thoughts for starting your sheets:

YOUR PENSIONS
- Find the current value of all your pensions. After 35 years of changing companies you may have an assortment of paid-up pensions from old employers, personal pensions, final salary pensions, and the state pension.
- The state pension is not exactly large to start with, but it could be even smaller if you haven't paid enough contributions. You may be advised to make extra ones to increase the final pension. Check with the Pensions Forecast Service (0845 3000168) on how much you can expect.

- For previous employer's pension schemes, if you have mislaid any policies or need help, get in touch with the Pension Tracing Service (0845 600 2357) who should be able to obtain details of any pension policy in the last 40 years. They will give you a valuation and your alternatives.
- You can get a valuation of your personal pension plans from the insurance company. You may not want to accept it now, but it will give you an indication of their current worth. You can then work out the value of the 25% you can take tax free, plus your income on current annuity rates.
- Don't forget that, when you really do decide to cash in, then you can take it to the market for competitive annuity offers. Best thought is to use a specialist annuity agency, which can advise on phased retirement, splitting your pension into mini-pension portfolios, or switching it into an income drawdown scheme. At the least, they will find you the best annuity going, and at no cost to you.

HOMES & FURNITURE
- Get a valuation of your principal home from a local estate agent, and then make allowance for all the costs of selling, from estate agent fees, government duty, lawyer's fees, to removals, new services, etc.
- Obtain a valuation on any second home, making allowances for all deductions for the usual costs, and not forgetting any capital gains tax.
- Obtain a valuation of all furniture and personal items such as jewellery, watches etc. This is worth doing, not only in case you want to sell one home with the furniture, but also to find out what potential income there might be from individual objects, should you ever need some money.

INVESTMENTS
- Make a list of all your share investments with their current value. Where it applies, note when any investment can be sold, and what it is expected to be worth at that date.
- Make a second list of all your savings, again noting when each can be sold. This list should include any moneys in

Isas, Tessas, PEPs, investment bonds, all fixed interest products, building society savings accounts, and any savings that are income producers.

CASH
- Check the amounts in all your bank accounts
- Check under every mattress

DEBTS
- Detail any outstanding loans from banks, other financial institutions, and individuals
- Make a list of any credit card balances to pay
- Obtain amount outstanding on any mortgages or re-mortgages, showing annual amounts and date of final payment

INCOME
- Payments from employers or clients
- Income from personal, private sources
- Income from dividends
- Interest due from savings accounts

EXPENDITURE
- Work out basic household budget, including food and drink, heat and light, clothes and beauty, holidays and cars, telephones and computer services, entertainment and entertaining, newspapers and TV services
- Bring forward the costs of your Grand Plan that you have already established.

At this point you should have a clearer idea of your wealth, both as of today, and in the future. You should know the value of your property and of your investment portfolio. You will know where all your savings accounts are and how much they total. And you will have found any forgotten cash.

For your cash flow you will know how much your expenditure is expected to be in the next, say, five years, and whether your existing revenue will cover it.

For most of us this is an exhausting experience. It takes time, if only because so many of us have never done it before. I know of friends who have easily taken over nearly a month to get the first clear picture on the screen of their financial position; and then continued to refine it over months.

Do you really need to do this exercise and go through the agony of producing reasonably accurate figures? I believe it is indispensable to a happy and successful Third Act for these reasons.

Eight Reasons for making Serious Budgets for Your Third Act

1. You need to know if your existing money will see you through the next 20 years; these are not years for money worries or a serious panic a decade down the road. If it doesn't, then you need to decide how you will obtain more income.

2. It gives you a chance to review all your savings accounts. Some may not be giving you the return you need; some may be totally wrong; some may no longer be tax efficient.

3. It is an opportunity to review all your share investments that may have been accumulated haphazardly over the years. You may want to change the balance of risk, or the sectors invested in.

4. Once you know the position on all your pensions, you are able to decide if it is better for your future finances to make further contributions to any of them, or to end them.

5. You may find that some furniture or jewellery is far more valuable than you realised, and could produce a significant inflow of new cash, when needed.

6. You will be able to decide on your property portfolio, and its possibilities as a future source of capital through re-mortgaging.

7. Your future budget predictions will show you whether you need to set up new long-term investments to mature 10 years on, such as 10-year bonds or Buy to Let flats.

8. Finally, this financial audit, this revealing of your actual financial worth, symbolises your take over of your life. You now know all the financial facts of your life, whether they be better or worse than you expected, and can plan to make the best use of them.

   You know now how much money you need in order to carry out your Grand Plan, how much may be needed to keep it going, and what moneys you have available to invest for the long term. You are now finally in charge of your future financial life.

I hope that these reasons are enough to convince you that it is worth taking up the challenge to enter your Third Act with a clear knowledge of your finance. You have so many good years ahead, and the better planned they are, the more happiness they will bring you.

QUESTIONS

1. Will your future income match your on-going liabilities?

2. Will you need to organise more money from some other source? *(See Chapters 14, 15, and 16)*

3. What do you expect your biggest shock will be, when you have done your financial audit?

CHAPTER 8

"Old age ain't no place for sissies."

H L Mencken

Don't Stop Working

Never say the R word. It may have been viable
50 years ago, but old-fashioned retirement
today is no longer a choice

O f all the thoughts in this book, this is one of the most important. Some of you might now start to question my sanity, but believe me, whatever your age, don't stop working. It may seem the dream to which you have worked your entire life, but if you don't find something to keep you busy and alert mentally, then you can soon find yourself slipping into the morning television shows.

Work less, of course, even far less, by all means. Work at a different job and work with different people, if that's what you want. Stay with the old company but on a different basis, if you prefer. But never completely stop working.

It is total nonsense to be working one week until Friday afternoon, and then suddenly stop, have a last drink with colleagues, and leave work, never to return. Come Monday morning you have nowhere to go; no one wants you. You are on your own in the world of No Work, for which you have no training.

For a few months you may enjoy the change, get up an hour later, see your partner more, play some golf, do odd jobs round the house, tidy up the garden, visit friends, or take a holiday. Maybe the pleasure of doing nothing is appealing for a while, but sociologists now confirm that it rarely lasts a year.

By that time, most people find it difficult to return to any work. They have lost that coterie of colleagues, and, worst of all, when the moment comes that they realise they are going to need more money – because the funds are running low, or they desperately need to get out of the house – many no longer have the confidence in their own abilities to find work. They find the retired life unsatisfactory, but very few can break back into the work force after so long away.

That is why I say 'Don't Stop Working', and have proposed that, in your Grand Plan for the Third Act of your life, you include some work from the very beginning. Of course, you will not want to go on working in anything like the same way as the previous 30 odd years. Nor am I suggesting that.

What I am suggesting is that some work is an integral part of the balance of your new life, where you aim to achieve your ambitions and enjoy your indulgences. How large that part is depends on your plan, but reduce it gradually, so that there is no sudden lurch out of the workplace.

The reality to remember is that retirement in the old-fashioned sense is simply no longer a viable alternative. It might have been fine 50 years ago, but anyone in their fifties today has at least another 20 years of a good life ahead – maybe 30 – so why waste them?

The idea of retirement for a year or so, as originally planned, made sense. Even for the expected five years it could have been a pleasant way of spending the last years, but, for twenty years and more in length, the concept of retirement is nonsense.

The idea of Retirement was a revolutionary concept when it was proposed by David Lloyd George. Bismark in Germany had suggested the idea that there was an age when people should stop working a few decades before, and Lloyd George imported it into England in 1911. By the age of 70 everyone had done their bit for the Empire, he decided, and they should, then, have the right to stop working and receive a State pension.

As usual with politicians, this was not as generous as it seemed, as the average age of life, for those who survived the first five childhood years, was 69. Lloyd George did not, therefore expect to pay out to many people.

The Attlee Government after the Second World War took up Lord Beveridge's recommendation to advance the age of a pension entitlement to 65. Again this was not expected to be excessively costly for the State, as people still, on average, lived to 69, and the Government expected to pay out no more than four or five years' pensions.

They saw no reason ever to budget for more, but, as usual with politicians, they got it wrong. Medical advances changed the odds. Antibiotics dramatically increased survival in the first five years of life; greater hygiene cut back on infections spreading; and scientists doubled medical knowledge every three years. As a result, life expectancy increased on average by two years every decade.

Then, sadly, just at the moment in history when we were all beginning to live longer, ageism dumped a whole generation onto the unemployed list, where they were regarded as unemployable and not needed.

This, happily, can never happen again. From October 2006 ageism is deemed to be illegal in the United Kingdom. After that, no staff can be forced to retire before 65 on grounds of age; training can not be denied to anyone because of their age; and no positions can be advertised specifying any particular age.

It is at least a start and it has taken a long time coming. It was 31 years earlier that the Sex Discrimination Act was passed, and that Act made discrimination on the grounds of sex or marriage unlawful. A year later The Race Relations Act outlawed any discrimination on the grounds of colour, race, nationality, or ethnic origin.

But it took another 30 years before Age Discrimination was outlawed. In that time a whole generation was discarded into various forms of retirement and out of the work place. In a mad epidemic of ageism millions were cut down in their prime, with the result that by 2006 only some six million of the 20 million people over 50 continued to work.

This extraordinary aberration of history was often justified by the belief that the ending of work and its replacement by Retirement was a 'good thing.' We now know differently, and the good news is that society is changing.

Millions have made it clear that they don't want to stop

working at any particular age. They do not want to continue full time for ever, as they have other ambitions to achieve, but they would be very happy to work part-time, so long as they were not penalised by tax for doing so.

In response to this, companies are now preparing to change their structure and their attitudes to work patterns, as the tax and pension confusion is cleared up. What is happening in the best of companies is that they now accept that people of any age can be retrained with new skills if necessary.

They are prepared to extend the practice of flexi-working to cover not merely hours but days, so that four and three day weeks are possible. They are happy to offer schemes whereby you can retire gradually, reducing, over several years, the amount of time spent working for the company. They will allow certain staff to contract their services as an outside consultant to the company.

In fact, most forward looking organisations now realise that their previous attitude to people working on into their sixties and later was almost entirely wrong.

This is why you now are able to plan to include work in your Grand Plan. A new law and a new attitude to older working is changing the business world.

Ten Reasons for Keeping on Working (But not full-time)

If you still have any doubt as to continuing to work, let me outline briefly why I believe work is a fundamental ingredient in your Grand Plan.

1. **We are essentially working and social animals**. We need the contact and familiarity with others, we need the companionship of shared activities, we are hunters who need to bring back something from the hills.

   We also need in some way to be identifiable. When you meet people, they tend to ask what you do. If you do nothing, what do you say? A job is not just an income, it is a social connection to mainstream life.

2. **You have no experience in leading a life with no work to do**. For 35 or more years you have worked for 40 to 50 hours a week. In England, we work more hours than anywhere else in the world. We have no siestas, we don't even have a good lunch nowadays. We go on grinding out the hours, five days a week for 46 weeks a year. Then suddenly you have nothing to do. No one has ever trained you to do nothing, and most people find the change difficult. No wonder that the dream of 'retirement' quickly soured for millions in the last generation.

3. **You may need to earn more money**. Some people can survive well enough, but the vast majority of us soon learn that we need more than we'd planned, especially now that we are going to live much longer. Keep the money coming in, so long as you need it. It probably will be less than before, because, on average, salaries peak in the mid-fifties, even for those in fulltime work. For you in part-time work, the pay will obviously be less. This doesn't matter. You are in the work community, you are still needed, your contribution is acknowledged.

4. **You want to live longer**. Stopping work is simply not good for you. According to the BMA, those who spend their last years doing no work are likely to die, on average, six years before those who do some work. In America the average is five years less life.

5. **You want to be healthier**. Those who give up work have more illness during their last decade. To lead a full life at any age, you need to exercise your mind and body, and it becomes even more important with each year from 50 onwards. Work is not the only way to do this, but it is a good start.

6. **You need to keep your network of friends**. In your Third Act you need a support group even more than before. You need to be out in the world keeping in touch with old friends; you need to have a happy home life. The divorce figures for those who give up work and hang around the home are a warning that your marriage might work better with your going out to work at least some days a week.

7. **All play and no work doesn't work**. We are perverse beings, but play is often only fun if it contrasts with work. If we can play golf every day, for example, then it becomes boring and even hard work. If we can play golf only on the days that we don't work, then it is fun. There is something in us that needs a contrast. Equally, all play and no work makes us far less interesting. It doesn't matter how glamorous your 'play' may be, or how extravagant, people who do nothing become very boring.

8. **You need to retain your self-esteem**. The way you go through life, the way you behave towards others, the confidence that you bring to your family often reflects the self-esteem in which you hold yourself. However pleased you are with the progress of other plans, maintaining a contribution in the work place is for many people part of their image of themselves and of their self-esteem.

9. **Business needs you**. Staying on at work has not been easy for the last couple of decades, while ageism has run rampant and too many companies made it difficult to continue working part-time.

   But that is changing. The new thinking – which was always obvious, but somehow ignored – is that the continuing employment of older people is 'a good thing', and to the benefit of the company. Why?

   • It reduces turnover costs because older people stay longer with their employer than younger ones

- It improves mentoring capacity, so that new young workers can be better trained by the older ones

- It maintains a wider staff base for dealing with customers of all ages, because many of them prefer to work with people of their own age

- It retains skills learnt over years of work

- It reduces absenteeism costs, because older people take off less days a year than younger ones

- It retains experience, which can never be replaced

Business now needs your experience. You need to work; they need you to work. Not full time, but enough for both sides to benefit. Both sides win.

10. **The Government also needs you**. The £30 billion bill that ageism added to social security payments can't go on extending. Even Whitehall is beginning to realise that they need your contribution to the Exchequer, and want to bring millions more into working life, who will pay more tax into the Treasury coffers.

They are beginning to wake up to this social revolution, and are planning to change the tax laws, so that working on is encouraged, not penalised.

As both Government and Business fully accept the advantages of allowing part-time working as a means of retaining the skills and experience of older staff, so you will be able more easily to include some work in your Grand Plan.

One of the reasons why I have argued that there has never been a better time to start your Third Act is that the bad old days of ageism are numbered. It is not exactly rocket science to see that a continuation in the work place by millions of people will fill the Government's black holes, increase corporate profitability, and enable everyone to include some work in their Grand Plan.

It is naive to think that all attitudes will change overnight, but they will change fast, and working part time is already the norm for one in five of the working population. The barriers are down, and you will be able to combine work alongside the other ambitions in the Grand Plan for your Third Act.

QUESTIONS

1. To keep working in your Third Act, will you stay with your company or set up your own consultancy?

2. Will you want to continue with the same work, or are you planning to change careers?

3. What changes do you believe the Government should make in taxation on income for those in their Third Act?

CHAPTER 9

*"No one should ever be quite accurate about their age.
It looks so calculating."*

Oscar Wilde

How Long Will You Live?

It gets longer every year – but how long
depends a lot on you

Something happened some 50 years ago that affects every one of us. Our life expectancy started accelerating. No scientist is quite certain why it happened, or whether it will inevitably continue, but right now our life expectancy continues to rise.

At 55 you're expected to live at least until 75. If you are reasonably fit at 60, your official Life Expectancy is 78; by 65 you're expected to enjoy another 15 years to 80. Once you reach 70 years, you are expected to live to 83, and half of us could have at least five years after that.

According to the great expert on the science of ageing, Professor Tom Kirkwood, our life span has increased by around two years every decade since the 1950s. And he sees no sign of it stopping. Our children will expect to live into their eighties, and many into their nineties.

Medical science is the largest cause of our longer survival. Medical knowledge, as I wrote previously, now doubles every three years, and, by the end of a decade, doctors expect to be able to begin rebuilding our immune systems, so that we become immune to many of the diseases that once struck particularly at older bodies.

Already we've seen major affects of immunisation in stopping once fatal diseases. At the beginning of the last century the main causes of death were influenza, diarrhoea, whooping cough, measles, TB and pneumonia. They are no longer the great killers that culled so many children until the 1950s.

Spare parts surgery can already replace anything from a heart to a hip. Scientists have already produced equivalent human life spans of a century in animals, and now claim to have the technology to translate this to humans.

Today the main causes of death are heart disease, cancer and strokes, but deaths even from these have been halved in the last 50 years. If scientists found an answer to the dreaded trio, then your life expectancy would rise to a century.

Your children may well live that long without any dramatic discoveries, as other advances come into the mainstream of medical practice. Gene therapy will correct gene defects; cell transports will grow new heart and brain tissue; hormonal replacement therapy will hold ageing at bay.

This is how some medical scientists see the future, but for us, right now, how long we will live depends much on us. No one is yet quite certain why the body ages. It was once accepted that the length of our life depended on our genes. The belief was that we have a biological clock that brings inevitable wearing out – from declining vision and hearing to weakening of the arteries and wearing out of the bones.

The Genetic argument is that we are all born with our own self-destruct programme. Our life is spelt out in our DNA, and our body simply follows its predetermined life span.

Today that belief is rejected. At most, it is now believed, genes make up only some 30% of the factors that affect our life; the other 70% depends on what we do to our minds and bodies.

These Wear and Tear theorists suggest that we cause much of our own health by abusing our bodies. Not necessarily by great excess, but simply by feeding our body with the wrong food, wounding it with nicotine and alcohol, and letting it weaken with lack of use. In their view, after a certain period our body loses its ability to repair the damage, and then the trouble starts.

So there's your decision right there. Do you accept the Geneticists' view that it's all in the genes and, therefore, you can do nothing about the length of time you live? Or, do you try and stave back the years?

If you decide to try for a longer life, I suggest that, at some point, you open the Web and take a longevity test. Just google *'how long will I live?'* and go through the tests. Some are jokey; some very serious. All are designed to give you an idea of how long you might live, if you carry on living the way you are now. The good tests take time, sometimes half an hour, but there's no point in hurrying them or hiding the truth. They are for your eyes only, and you will decide what you want to do after going through them.

The most unexpected thing I found is that they all seem to agree within a few years. Presumably because they are often based on the same actuary tables or the same medical views, but even the jokey ones finished up with the same figure as the long tests.

Choose whichever catches your attention, but don't miss *northwestern mutual, livingto100.com*, and particularly *realAge*, because it is as dogmatic as it is informative. Created by Dr. Michael Roizen, it gets about 12 million hits a year, and he leaves you in no doubt that you can change how long you will live. He reckons that there are 125 prime factors that affect our ageing, and his test takes all of them into account.

The Silver Wolf Ten Commandments for Living Longer

It isn't just the length of time you may live, but about the quality of your life. If you have a lot of dreams to fulfil, and intend to lead a full life for another 25 years at least, then there's no point in letting your mind and body deteriorate to such an extent that you don't enjoy this longevity.

Here then are the *Silver Wolf* guidelines for living not just long, but well. Some are obvious and some are the usual suspects, but together they should add many years to your life.

- **Keep your weight to within 5% of your ideal size**
- **Keep your blood pressure down**
- **Eat and drink less**
- **Don't smoke**
- **Take physical exercise daily**
- **Stretch your mind daily**
- **Avoid stress**
- **Surround yourself with loving people**
- **Laugh and smile**
- **Think young and positive**

1. **Keep your weight to within 5% of your ideal size**. You know how much, according to the medical tables, that your weight should be for your height. Note it down, together with the figures for 5% more or less. Check your weight every week, so that any change can be stopped before it gets too much.

2. **Aim to keep your blood pressure low**. Low blood pressure reduces your chances of a heart attack or stroke. If you climb above 140/100, work with your doctor on ways to bring it down quickly. Ask him about aspirin, which some doctors swear should be part of our daily ritual,

3. **Go Mediterranean**. Eat and drink your way through the next 20 years in what sociologists call the *style de la Med*. Eat less red meat and more fish. Drink only red wine, water, and no spirits. Use olive oil, and no saturated fat. Cook your own food, and never eat processed food, usually full of salt. Eat more fruit, nuts and vegetables, especially tomatoes and broccoli – we need the lycopene to keep the prostate healthy. Eat often and less, but take longer to do it.

4. **Don't smoke**. Totally obvious, and most people over 50 have now cut out smoking, but the effect on your immune system and arteries from passive smoke is now thought to be almost

as bad. Your lungs don't like it; nor does your throat and arteries. But cancer cells do, so avoid smoking areas.

5. **Take physical exercise every day**. This is a mantra that we've all heard a thousand times, but gerontologists say that it is almost like a magical pill as we get older. Exercise doesn't just make you feel better and look better, but, more importantly, it makes your body work better. It's like the car, they say, in an attempt to get us to understand; it lasts longer if it's constantly used, and, every now and then, it needs a good run.

    In our case, exercise obviously helps our cardiovascular system, and strengthens our muscles and bones, but, also, it helps slow down some of the damage that contributes to our ageing. Make aerobic exercise part of your normal life pattern.

    You should exercise in some way every day. Walk to work, ignore the lift, spend 10 minutes with the medicine ball, go dancing, do whatever you can.

6. **Stretch your mind**. Mental exercise is just as important as physical. The previous generation often thought there was little point, as they had been told that senility was inevitable, but all scientific tests comparing generations show that there need, in fact, be no change.

    Over the five areas of mental abilities – verbal meaning, word fluency, inductive reasoning, numerical ability and spatial orientation – different generations scored higher in different areas, but with no overall victor.

    Dr. Kawas, the gerontologist at John Hopkins, argues that we may lose some memory ability, but that is more than matched by a greater vocabulary, more ability to reason, and better judgement based on experience.

    Critical is the continuous of intellectual activity, which develops surplus brain tissue that compensates for the normal wear and tear. You don't need some anti-aging drug, but keep the mind challenged. If you don't keep it ticking over, then it will become weak and febrile.

All the mind asks is constant use from the morning cross-word to the evening dinner discussion. In between, do some work, learn a language, and enjoy some time with friends. Above all become a lifetime learner. Learning stretches your mind, and makes you more tolerant.

7. **Avoid Stress**. Stress has got to stop, if you want to live longer. It may have been a continuous part of your full-time working past, but it takes years off your life. However you create your new Grand Plan, make certain it can be done without stress. Absolutely nothing, according to the gerontologists, causes premature ageing more quickly. Anger causes more heart attacks than high cholesterol or being overweight.

    If you find urban life stressful, move to the country. On average, country dwellers, according to the Office for National Statistics, live eight years longer than townees.

8. **Surround yourself with love**. It may sound too much like a women's magazine, but happiness and contentment is a key to fulfilling your ambitions. You need love in your home, among your family, and with your friends; without their support, your achievements can seem hollow.

    Sort out differences, clear the air of past mistakes, and give more of yourself to those around you. Above all, learn to express your emotions; don't bottle them up.

    As for friends, welcome new ones, and renew contact with old ones, but keep only the cheerful ones. The grouches take the joy out of life; according to Yale University research, optimists live seven years longer than miserable people.

9. **Laugh and Smile**. It follows that, if you are surrounded with love, you will be happy. Then show it. Learn how to laugh again; find the amusing side of life, and don't grumble. No one is quite certain why laughter is such a healer, but it is. Laughter is believed to be one way of preventing heart attacks, and many people with cancer claim to have cured themselves by listening to their favourite comedians, and laughing out loud and often.

10. **Think young**. Create your Grand Plan, so that you are starting out on a new life, not closing down. You have the ambitions and positive attitude of a young man; you rediscover the excitement of learning again and achieving some dreams. You remember that you are only as old as you tell yourself, as young as you look, and as welcome as your smile.

And one extra commandment.

- **Don't die young**. Every day, doctors learn more, so, the later you need treatment, the more likely they are to be able to cure you. As an example, few surgeons in England were capable of dealing with prostate operations even 15 years ago; today treatment of this singularly male problem is better understood and far better handled.

In previous centuries, life expectancy increased from a combination of advances in sanitation, better understanding of nutrition, and the ability to detect and treat infectious diseases.

The result was that, by the beginning of the 20th century, those who survived the first five years of life could expect to live to 69.

By the beginning of this century, antibiotics, nutritional supplements, and greater surgical skills had extended, for those who reached school age, the average life expectancy to 79.

By the end of this century, some medical scientists are talking of extending a healthy life to an average of 89. Too late for us, but, nanotechnology and biotechnology may be only a decade away, so concentrate on staying healthy for a long time.

Medical scientists claim that by 2025 cancer will no longer be a killer, and that they will be able to slow down your DNA damage. From these experiments will come anti-ageing pills, with the possibility of extending healthy life to 100 years.

Above all, you know that you can influence not only the length of your life, but also its quality. You can take control of the way you live, and give yourself more time to fulfil your dreams.

QUESTIONS

1. How long do you want to live?

2. What changes in your life do you need to make to reach that age?

3. Which change will be the most difficult for you?

CHAPTER 10

"It's not how old you are, but how you are old."
Marie Dressler

Stay Healthy

If you're going to have a 20-year Grand Plan, it makes sense to ensure that you live long enough to enjoy it

L et's face it, nothing is more important than your health. It doesn't matter how cleverly you may have organised your money; how wisely you have arranged your working future; or how delicately you may have balanced you family affairs. Without your health you can't enjoy any of your Grand Plan.

The good news is that bad health is not inevitable in the Third Act. The bad news is that many of us have abused our bodies over the previous decades and need to change a few things. If you're now talking of a Grand Plan, when you plan to fulfil your dreams, and have the best years of your life over the next 20 or more years, then you want to be healthy, don't you?

What is important first is to realise that age does not inevitably brings illness. Here are six traditional myths about age and health, and they are all false.

Six Myths About Your Health

1. **Getting older automatically means getting ill. Not true**
   There is no physical or physiological reasons why anyone over 60 should expect to have more health problems that they did in the earlier years

2. **Older people's illnesses become a liability in the work force. Not true**

   In fact it is the opposite. Not only do we bring more knowledge and experience to our daily work, but we take far less time off. In fact we take less than in any decade, and far less than those in their thirties.

3. **Most people over 60 suffer from a serious chronic complaint. Not true**

   The last survey that came out as I was writing this book showed that 71% of us at 55–75 years were 'in fine form', and another 18% were alright.

4. **Most of us finish up in nursing homes. Not true**

   Contrary to the impression sometimes given in newspapers, less than 3% of us will ever find ourselves staying one night in a care home.

5. **Older people are a burden on the NHS. Not true**

   It is true that we can cost more from our eighties onwards, but not now. According to official figures, over 80% of NHS costs are incurred by all of us in the first five years of our lives, and then in the last year and a half. Not during the years of the Third Act.

6. **Our bodies deteriorate from 55 onwards. Not true**

   We actually start deteriorating from the mid-thirties! Nothing new happens in the mid-fifties, sixties or seventies. You have to work harder to keep your body healthy with each decade from the mid-thirties onwards, but, given some reasonable genes and some luck, your health need not change dramatically at any time throughout your whole Third Act.

That's the good news. The bad news is that your body may well need help, if it's going to keep going without trouble. Because what most of us did to our bodies in the great working Second Act, catches up on you from now on.

You need to take as honest a look at your body as you did in looking at your plans for your Third Act. You don't have to, of course. You can continue stuffing yourself with food the body doesn't want, drinking more alcohol than it can cope with, smoking out the lungs, walking no further than from the car to the house, but then don't be surprised when you spend your last decade in and out of hospital.

I exaggerate, but you know what I mean. Many of us enter our Third Act with bodies that have been badly treated, and there really doesn't seem much point in going on doing it.

It is clearly preferable to feel healthy, energetic and fit, if only to reduce the chance of getting any illnesses. You know that, if you don't change, you could lose a lot of good times with bad health, and lose a lot of years from dying earlier.

It is also clearly preferable to continue to be a healthy sexually attractive man. If you are genuinely appalled, when you stand full-length, naked in front of the mirror, and think to yourself, *"Thank heavens she can't see me now"*, then it's time to change. Sex is a powerful reason for change, whether you're looking for a new partner, or trying to keep the one you've got.

On a more practical level, you might quite like to be able to wear three-quarters of your wardrobe again, especially now most of it is back in fashion.

Whichever reason is yours for changing your life style, only you can make yourself fit and healthy again. No one can make you, so you have to decide, as early into your Third Act as possible, that you will change. Good intentions are not enough; you have to accept the following as part of your Grand Plan.

Your 10 Acceptances For a Long Healthy Life

1. **You accept the need to change, and get an MOT of your body**. This will give you a rundown on the general state of your body, weight, blood pressures, cholesterol level, body mass ratio and so on. This is your starting point, so that you

know the changes recommended by doctors to improve the state of your health.

2. **You accept the medical recommendations and agree to eat less, drink less, and exercise more**. At this stage you write down your targets in your personal diary and not for public eyes. Then you take private photos of yourself in the full length mirror in the bathroom. Every time you feel like going back to the old eating days, get the picture out as a reminder of why you're changing.

3. **You accept that obesity is a most dangerous enemy**. It cuts back your chances of living longer, and increases your chances of being ill. I have a friend who cheerfully carried two stone too much for 30 years and still won the club tennis championship. Then the body gave up the fight, his knees went, he had one hip bone replaced, and they're planning to do the other. He's now 64 and almost house-bound.

4. **You accept that smoking has to stop**. The evidence now is too strong to ignore. When you smoke, you are gambling with various forms of cancer, apart from breathlessness and bad breath. It is not hard to stop. Just stop. It's easiest to do this when you have a bad cold, as I found. Others found hypnotism worked.

5. **You accept that drinking a lot had better stop**. Drinking and smoking often went together, and it's easier to stop both together. Forget the cold turkey tales. The body's got used to its daily alcohol fix, but it can quickly get used to not having it.

    Two things happen. First, it finds that it prefers the water you pour down, because that's what it really does need. Second, it loses the ability to handle strong alcohol, and gives you a headache if you take much of it.

    The good news is that not even the most Calvinist doctor wants us to stop drinking completely. Up to three glasses of red a day is, apparently, actually good for us, and far better than drinking none. Not white wine, not spirits, but red wine. It's something to do with the resveratrol compound in it, which suppresses cancer cells.

6. **You accept that, from now on, you have to give the body what it wants as a basic diet.** What it wants every day is two litres of water, five portions of fruit and vegetables, 1,500 calories of proper food and drink, and 30 minutes of exercise.

7. **You accept that your toughest job is to 'tame the tum'.** The stomach is like a child who's been indulged. It's got used to all the food you've forced it to digest, and will go on asking for it, until it finally learns that you're not going to give it any more. Once it realises that, it will cease sending hunger demands to your brain, and you will stop feeling hungry.

8. **You accept the need to exercise.** Exercise after 50 is like a magic pill, so effective is it on our bodies.

9. **You accept that from now on you no longer live to eat, you eat to live.**

10. **You accept all this, because you want to enjoy your Third Act, and you want to look younger, healthier, and sexier.**

Getting your body healthy again isn't exactly rocket science. We all know that it consists of only one mantra. *Eat less, and exercise more. Eat less and exercise more. Eat less and exercise more.* And so on.

Nor do most of us have any excuse for knowing how to get fitter and healthier. Endless books and articles have gone on *ad nauseam* about dozens of conflicting diets, from *Calories don't count* to *Count the calories*, and all the exercises from pilates and yoga to swimming and running.

Go through a selection of diets, and find one that makes sense to you. I suspect it matters little what diet you follow. Diet advice changes by the year and no one is certain which fad is right.

What is important is what we all know.

Take in less, and take off more.

That is why I am *not* going to add to that list of diets in *Silver Wolf*. What follows is simply what I learnt, to solve my own problems. While my height stayed at 6'2", my weight has yoyo-ed most of my life. I have now been steady at 85 kilos for a decade, but at various times I have been between 75 and 95 kilos. I ate, smoked and drank too much in some of the early years. I put on jowls, a pair of love handles, and at one time breathed heavily just climbing the stairs to the children's floor.

I only mention that, to promise you that the thoughts that follow are not from some fitness freak, but solved real problems. They are not detailed reports on what you should eat or drink, but the approaches that might help.

And, they work.

The Silver Wolf 20 Starters on Eating and Drinking

1. **Don't go hungry**. Losing weight doesn't mean going hungry; it means eating better food. You know what better food means – more fruit and vegetables, no junk food, less meat, less fat and dairy, and more fish. It's not complicated.

2. **Cut out all your old food on Day One**. Don't wean yourself off things gradually, but empty out the refrigerator and cupboards, and start the first day of your new life.

3. **Don't try to follow any crazy diet**. Most of them don't work in the long term. Learn from them, but you work out your own eating pattern.

4. **Don't bother to count your calories at the start**. Whatever you're eating, halve it, and add on a lot more fruit and vegetables.

5. **Eat slowly**. Simple advice, but it made a difference for me. Much of the food we stuff into ourselves is often too awful to taste, like most sandwiches, so we eat quickly. Eat slowly, taste it, and you'll eat less and probably change your food for a better taste.

6. **Eat only when you're hungry**, and stop when you've had enough. Too often we eat by habit, when we really don't need to eat. Some of us, also from a childhood habit, feel we have to finish the plate. It's not necessary.

7. **Breakfast like a king, lunch like a prince, and dine like a pauper**. The old medical advice is still the best. Getting a decent meal in you to start the day is far better than a heavy meal at night. To eat practically nothing all day and then a lot at night is exactly what your body does not want, and won't help you become fitter and healthier.

8. **Eat nothing that can be eaten without utensils**. Another simple rule, but it cuts out any sandwiches, chocolates, ice-creams, biscuits, sweets, crisps, cakes, etc. The great exception to this is fresh fruit. When you feel hunger, or need what the psychologists call oral satisfaction, take a piece of fruit – grapes, bananas, apples, oranges, whatever you enjoy.

    For me, mandarins are the answer to solving the moments when I feel hungry. Every room in the house and office has this easy-to-eat fruit, which stops me finding something stupid to eat.

9. **Eat at least five portions of fruit and vegetables a day**. I know it's become the medical mantra, but it's good advice. The leafy vegetables, led by broccoli and spinach, and the root ones, like carrots and swedes, we all know about, but, to prevent heart diseases, also add onions, leeks, shallots and garlic. The French claim that garlic is the reason why they can enjoy rich dishes and still live longer than we do.

10. **Eat more white and less red meat**. Red meat is fine on occasion, but the belief now is that white is less heavy and better handled by our digestive systems,

11. **Make fish your main food**, especially the oily fish like salmon, tuna, mackerel, sardines and kipper. They have omega3 acids that help to thin the blood and prevent strokes.

12. **Add high-fibre grains** in whatever forms you can take them. These include brown rice, oatcakes, walnuts and cashews, pumpkin and sunflower seeds. These all reduce your cholesterol level and so help prevent heart problems.

13. **Drink more water**. Water is what the body craves, and we're supposed to take three litres a day. I find that difficult. A litre is easy, two is an effort, and three for me is impossible. But somehow we do need at least two litres a day to wash through the body.

    You may find that the easiest way to get this amount of water down is with juices. I mix the water with apple, fresh orange, or cranberry juice, all of which add to our immune systems, and especially non-pasteurised apple cider vinegar. This form of vinegar is just about the oldest health food in history, recommended by from Hippocrates downwards, and helps postpone the dreaded arthritis.

14. **Drink herbal teas**. When you, perhaps reluctantly, discard the fried egg and bacon on fried bread, forget the milky tea that went with it. All herbal teas are better for your digestion, and have a calming effect on your nerves.

    Some are an acquired taste, and none more so than green tea. I found it difficult to like this drink for a long time, but it's easier to take, now that there are green teas with fruit flavours.

    Green tea is another of those ancient healers, and the argument for it is strong. Its powerful EGCG anti-oxidant makes it the all-singing, all-dancing elixir that will kill cancer cells, lower cholesterol levels, and cut down the chances of blood clots. Not a bad promise, and it might even be true.

15. **Check on the value of your food**. Once you've broken your old habits and got your stomach's phoney hunger demands under control, learn a bit more about the contribution that various foods can give your body.

    You started by cutting down your intake to lose weight, but then comes the stage when it's worth checking that your body is getting enough minerals and vitamins in your new regime.

    As an obvious example, a pizza and half a bottle of red a day, totalling 1000 calories with nothing else, would certainly lose you weight for a while, but wouldn't do much for your body's health.

16. **Find a good pharmacist** or health shop that can give you knowledgeable advice on what mineral and vitamin supplements you may need. Be honest with them, and they can be of enormous help.

17. **Detox one day a week**. Make a practice of taking a Detox Day, when you have nothing but vegetables, fresh fruit, water and herbal teas.

18. **Give yourself a Treat** once a week, when you eat whatever you miss most – even if it's only an ice-cream or piece of chocolate.

19. **Don't panic**, if all your sacrifices seem to be in vain for a few weeks. You don't want to lose weight too fast. A pound a week will do. Remember that the weight drops off first from the top and then moves down, so your stomach and love handles are the last to go.

20. **Celebrate** when you reach your target weight, and make a toast, vowing never to gain more than five pounds above that weight ever again.

E ating less and eating better food will certainly bring down your weight. It will also help your body organs to function better, because you are not asking them to work with foods they don't need, but are giving them foods with the vitamins and minerals they do need.

But, losing weight won't make you fit, nor make your body as healthy as it wants to be. To achieve that, you need to exercise. Many of us walk little, run rarely, and exercise only on protest. We give up our sport too young, and are surprised when we fail to finish the parents' dash on Sports Day.

Somehow, we have to change all that, put the clock back, and get our body back. Here are ten thoughts for those whose lives have become too busy to work out, and need to start again.

The Silver Wolf 10 Thoughts on Getting Fit

1. **Exercise every day.**
   It's better to do a little exercise every day than one long workout a week. Carve out 30 minutes every day to do something that makes your body work. Put it in your diary, so that it becomes as official and important as your meetings.

2. **Vary your exercise**.
   So long as you do 30 minutes, you can do whatever is convenient for you each day. Walk a brisk three miles, play squash, do the Canadian Air Force exercises, make passionate love. Anything that gets your heart beating, your body sweating, and tests your endurance.

3. **Exercise at home**.
   Buy a large medicine ball and roll around on that. My gym instructor swears that this is all you need to start with. Use it for 15 minutes each morning, lying on it, sitting on it, and using it against the wall to strengthen your thighs and knees.

4. **Run up and down the stairs, wherever you can.**
   Run up and down the stairs in your house, as well as your office building. There is strong evidence that people who live

in flats have twice as much illness after 55 than those who live in houses. It's the stairs that make the difference. Running up stairs exercises your heart and strengthens your leg muscles.

5. **Swim a lot**.
Swimming uses more of your body than you would imagine, According to the fitness guru at my club, if we only had time to do one thing a day, swimming is the most useful. If you don't like the public baths and aren't near the sea, join a club with a good pool.

6. **Join a Health Club**.
Millions join; only thousands use it after a few months. Find a good one, join by the month, and get the instructors to work out your personal programme. Only a health club will have all the facilities you will need when you're ready to be serious. At a good club you can do the circuit, build your strength with weight training, row, cycle, swim, learn Capoeira, join a Pilates group, fence, all among others with similar targets as you.

7. **Get a Personal Trainer**.
They make certain you are doing the right exercises for you, that you actually do them, and that you make real progress. You make certain you can work with the person. My first personal trainer was an ex-sergeant and treated all his clients like new recruits. We soon parted, and I was recommended to a girl, who was just as vicious, but smiled while she nearly broke my back. Good Personal trainers don't come cheap, but they're worth it.

8. **Trust your body**.
Don't ever think that your body is too old to do something. Your mind may think that, but the body is willing. Too old for tennis at 55? Not true, look at the over-50s tournaments. Too old for a marathon at 60? Not true; look at the London Marathon lists. Once you have brought your body back to fitness, you can do most things.

9. **Enjoy using your body again**.
   Being fit is not a passing campaign, but will gradually become a normal way of living. And when does that happen? When you can run without feeling exhausted. When you actually enjoy walking to the station. When your old clothes actually fit. When your old friends ask how you can stay so young. When that picture of you starkers in the bathroom, taken the day you started, now looks like someone else!

10. **Don't give in**.
    Don't ever slip back into your old ways; enjoy your new pattern of eating and drinking habits. Keeping your body healthy is an ongoing part of your Third Act, not a three month wonder. You've taken the decision to get fit again for a number of reasons, but the most important is that you are getting fit for a long and healthy life.

It is often difficult to start a healthy life after years of letting the body go. Anyone who tells you it is easy is lying. It is a challenge and will need all your courage and determination.

But it is worth it in so many ways. It will improve your health. It will prolong your enjoyment of living. It will make you younger not just in appearance, but also in your attitude and confidence. And it will make you more sexy. Not a bad deal.

QUESTIONS

1. What exercises will you choose to help you to live long and stay healthy?

2. What changes will you make in your life patterns?

3. Which foods will you change?

4. Do you wish you hadn't read this chapter?

CHAPTER 11

"I still enjoy sex at 75. I live at 76, so it's no distance."
Bob Monkhouse

Nothing Better Than Sex

Don't think of England, think of your health

You've got to admit that this is the best chapter heading yet, but what does it mean? Well, it means that, if you want to keep healthy, fit, happy and young in your Third Act, then regular sexual activity is a great help. Whatever else is in your Grand Plan, sex has to be included.

The good news is that many of us already know that and do our best: even better news is that sex is not only enjoyable, but the best natural therapy we have.

Two massive surveys in America and Europe sent a clear rebuttal to the myth that sex has no part in later lives. They claimed that not only is a great deal of sex going on, but it is better than it has been for decades.

The greatest years, according to these surveys, were 18–35, when over 70% declared that they have a good or satisfactory sex life. The end of sexual life as we know it came quickly for those in their Second Act, when two-thirds of them declared, with refreshing honesty, that they had a pretty rotten sex life. Among the 35–55s, only 32% thought their sex life was even remotely satisfactory.

Presumably this collapse of sexual life can be blamed on stress at work and the children at home. These 20 years may be the best financially, but are equally often the worst in personal relationships. Good old-fashioned lust hardly flourishes with a briefcase of work on the dining table and noisy children in every other room.

Whatever the reason, life gets better with the years. In the 55

Plus group nearly 60% of those in their Third Act told the pollsters that their sex life was satisfactory, thank you. Some even said it was the best ever.

So, that kills off any idea that sex might end once the fifties arrived; in fact it actually restarts for a third of the families. But how do we know it is more enjoyable? From anecdotal evidence only, but there's so much of it that it's almost believable.

According to women, men become '*less rushed*', '*more caring*', '*more skilful*', and '*more cuddling.*' According to men, women become '*more active*', '*more certain what they want*' and '*more grateful*'. The last comment seems a tad ungallant, but it occurred so often that it was clearly an important reaction.

Even if you take this kind of survey with a large pinch of proverbial salt, the very least it confirms is that sex is alive and well and flourishing far better among the over-55s than it does for those 15 years younger.

The More Sex the Better

How times have changed. I remember my mother gently mocking an old school friend, who confided in her that she had told her husband that they were '*now too old for all that*'. The friend was 57 at the time, and looked a great deal older.

Today, her doctor would tell her that she was neither too old for sex, nor should she deny herself the youthfulness it can prolong. If you believe the medical profession today, having sex is almost a duty, because of the amount of good it can do to our body and mind. Why is that? Four reasons.

- "*Regular sex keeps your cardiovascular system in good order, and is the first thing I recommend to my patients*", said the late transplant surgeon, Christian Barnard, who knew a bit about these matters, both personally and professionally.
  "*Sex is the most beautiful and pleasurable way to keep the circulation in gear, and keep your heart healthy,*" he taught. "*Regular sex helps to maintain your blood pressure at a lower rate.*"

At first hearing, this sounds nonsense, because we all know that our blood pressure rises during sex, and so does our heart rate. But after sex it falls even lower than before, and so you progressively lower your blood pressure every time you have sex.

As heart attacks are the second largest cause of death after cancer, even my mother's old friend would now not have to think of England, but could dream of her falling blood pressure.

- Sex in some medical circles is also called the 'secret health and fitness weapon'. Many people begin to go pear-shaped after a certain age, not because of the years weighing heavily on them, according to some doctors, but from lack of sexual activity.

  It is sex that releases hormones, like adrenaline, that break down glucose rather than storing it as fat. A hundred hours of enthusiastic sex a year will, according to the new thinking, reduce those masculine love handles and tone up feminine thighs.

  My wife's doctor is a new bachelor and a car fanatic, who prides himself on having the best-tuned Alvis TD21 convertible in the district. He explains the importance of sex to his patients in a motoring analogy.

  "Sex is too important to stop. Your heart system needs a good workout every week. It's like taking the car for a good run to get all the parts working properly. You can get your heart pounding by going on a five mile jog, or you can do it with half an hour's love-making. It's up to you."

  "After the menopause, sex can initially be difficult for some women because their natural secretions dry up. For some men, inflammation of the prostate puts them off sex, but all these conditions are treatable. Whatever the problem, don't give in to it."

- Sex is also at work on the brain, where it releases endorphins. Known as 'happy' hormones, they, at the least, reduce stress levels and depression. At their best they give us that happy look that radiates out of people in love.

- Sex can give us a longer life. A recent Edinburgh survey showed that, certainly in that elegant city, those who enjoyed at least one orgasm a week were twice as likely to reach their expected age, than those who had only one a month. Research in Stockholm suggested that a good sex life usually made people in their Third Act look five years younger.

The Sexual Performance

All this is very well, you may be thinking, but all is sometimes not totally well in the performance department. The spirit is willing, but there are certain problems. Fear not, you are not alone,

Let's get the bad news out of the way first. You have been losing your libido since the day of your 20th birthday. From then on it has been downhill all the way. After the age of 30 your testosterone levels has dropped by about 1% a year. Even so, by the age that you start your Third Act, you have only lost some 25%, and should have no lack of facial hair, muscle development or an interest in sex.

Women's libido peaks at 30, but their problems get worse at the menopause. After that, one in three women go off sex. One out of three are happy to return to it; but the other one in three are even more eager for it.

That's their problem; ours are technical problems that affect some men's views of themselves as macho men, but really aren't serious. They are:

- **Erectile Dysfunction**, sometimes known as Brewers Droop, colloquially known as an inability to get it up, and abbreviated to ED. Join the club. Half the men from 40 onwards have this problem at some time.

  It comes partly from clogging arteries, which prevent the right amount of blood being pumped into the penis; partly from your mind, because you are worried and tired; and partly from your habits. So, cut back immediately on the booze, cut out smoking, check any pills you may be taking, and stop worrying. Within a month you should be a different man.

- **Slow to climax**. Who cares? Your partner should be delighted that you no longer come in six minutes, as you did at 40. She might at last get some pleasure from it. The time it takes us to climax goes like this: three minutes at 20, 6 at 40, 12 at 50, 18 at 60 and 24 at 70 years. I'm not certain of the validity of this research, but that's what the sexologists tell us.

- **Not much sperm produced**. So what? After the age of 50 the amount of semen we produce is not very generous – an egg cupful at best, a teaspoon more usually. Nor does it travel far. No longer the gush of early youth, more an inch or two. That's normal and of no worry to either side. Taking a hot bath before sex makes it worse, as the sperm-making cells don't work properly, unless they are cooler than body temperature.

- **Just won't perform**. OK, this might need help, and the doctor can supply it. Viagra is the most famous drug, but Cialis, Tadalafil, and Levitra might suit you better. No longer a sniggering joke, drug treatment for ED is now in the public arena,

  Sir Stirling Moss had the prostate operation that millions of men have, and found that ED happened to him. He now fronts a campaign to make us all aware of the drugs that can help. For him, by the way, it is Levitra, which only takes 10 minutes to get off the grid.

Finding a Partner

The other slight technical hitch might be the fact that you currently don't have a partner. Not surprising. Divorce is spreading like a rash across the face of the fifty-year-olds, and just over one in three of the single households in Britain is now over 50. Welcome to the world of the singletons. This is your world:

- If you believe the official estimates, there are some three million over 55 living alone, and learning to restart lives without a partner in the home. You are not alone. You are not even a rarity.

- The good thing to remember is that there are three times as many women looking for a mate than there are men. I cannot understand how that works out, but it is apparently true.

- If you want a new partner – dreadful word – you'll have to learn, all over again, after decades of not bothering, where and how to find one. The where is the same and obvious. At work; at sports clubs and gyms; at local cafes and hotel bars; at evening classes; at hobby clubs; even in the vegetable section at Sainsburys. More obvious advice is to consider where a woman, with the same interests as you, might go, and be there.

- An easy start can be made through the Personal pages in the papers. Once the home of slightly dubious propositions, you will be amazed at the eclectic advertisers now looking for a mate.

- If all else fails, you'll find the world is now full of dating agencies. They can arrange to give your details to an endless number of potential mates. There may be an agency around the corner from you, and there are certainly some on the web. Google *over 50s dating services,* for a selection.

- Whatever you do, keep going out. Women may be much more forward than they were when you last dated, but they don't yet come knocking on your door. Join clubs, accept all invitations, keep yourself on show. And stop looking married; women are more usually looking for a pair bonding, not an affair.

Silver Wolf Top Ten Dating Tips

However you find a potential partner, you'll want to remind yourself how the game is played. Truth to tell it hasn't changed all that much. Both of you will be nervous at the first meeting; both of you will be hoping that this time it is the right person. Both of you will probably think afterwards that you made a mess of the meeting.

Dating again after a long time is not easy, and you may get it wrong for some time. You're out of practice, you're not certain what you're doing there, and you may feel like the proverbial duck out of water. You will probably feel more nervous with a woman than at any time since you were last a bachelor, maybe 30 years ago.

It can be ghastly for the first few months, so here are some tips for those revisiting the dating game after decades of marriage.

1. **Don't worry about your age**. In fact, don't talk about age. You're both going to lie anyhow. Remind yourself that most women like a man to be older. This doesn't mean you should look or behave like old men used to. She wants to be assured that you have at least 20 more good years in you.

2. **Look your best**. Don't ignore the sartorial changes of the last couple of decades, but don't ape them. You don't have to wear trainers, jeans, leather jacket and T-shirt. Equally, you don't have to stick to cords, check shirt, tie and jacket. Dress in the way that makes you feel most confident, but for heavens sake wear fresh clothes and look smart. Nothing puts a woman off quicker than seeing her new date come through the doors in dirty, scruffy clothes.

3. **Stand tall**. You know, like Big John Wayne did, or Sean Connery does. Head up and shoulders back gives that confident powerful look that many women enjoy. Too many men drop into a slouch, as they get older; don't join them.

4. **Make her laugh**. Smile and be amusing. Women will forgive a great deal if you make them laugh, and don't take yourself too seriously. I don't recommend your telling jokes, but just show that you have a sense of humour, and can be amusing. If you do make a joke, make it against yourself.

5. **Compliment her**, and make her feel relaxed. Remember, she's probably as nervous as you are. Few people bother to compliment others, but we all welcome a touch of praise, and are grateful for it.

6. **Listen to her**. Ask her questions. Before your old marriage ended, you'd probably long given up listening to your partner. Truth be known, that was one cause of the break up. Now learn to listen. Look at her when she's talking, and at least pretend to be interested.

7. **Don't go on about your past**, and never about four things: your ex-wives, ex-girl friends, the old days, and illnesses – especially your prostate. You are a successful, attractive and happy man, who is meeting this woman for a possible new future. Forget the past.

8. **Don't rush things**. Relationships need time to grow, and, even if there's little chemistry, you might welcome a new friend. Besides, the second meting might show that she has far more virtues than you realised at first.

9. **Don't give up**. If the first dates are disasters, what have you lost? Just a couple of hours. Think of them as practice for the day when you meet the right one.

10. **Behave like the gentleman you are**. There aren't many of us left, and, contrary to yob myth, most women still prefer to be treated as ladies.

If your dating is getting desperate and you do ever feel like giving up the search for some loving sex, don't.

To listen to some medics talk about sex sometimes, you'd think they'd just discovered the answer to the Mystery of the Universe. But they are only typical of the New Thinking that credits sex with having more good results than all the scanning equipment in the local hospital.

Just to remind you, according to this view, a regular sex life can work the following miracles:

- **It can reduce your blood pressure**
- **It can reduce your stress**
- **It can change your shape**
- **It can change the way you look facially**
- **It can radiate a happy aura**
- **It can extend your life**

It doesn't look a bad deal. Whatever else the Great Plan has, a regular sex life should be there somewhere. It may require some changes being agreed by both parties, and the two of you may not always have the same timing, but clearly the doctors can't all be wrong.

As an unchangeable romantic I'm not certain that this 'happy aura' can't also come from a loving relationship where two people are simply still in love, and it is apparent to the whole world. I have friends who clearly rediscovered each other, once the children had left the family nest, and they look younger, and better, than they ever did 10 years ago.

I don't think they have quite rediscovered the do-it-anywhere-anytime lust of early love, but I do know they talked together about their sexual relationship, as part of the Grand Plan for the rest of their Third Act. The result is usually a quieter kind of lovemaking that is as much giggles as gurgles, and certainly less gymnastic.

Even if the response is not always what is expected, it can usually be worked out amicably. Do you remember the classic story of a chap who had an unpleasant heart attack, which left him *hors de combat* for a few months. Then one day he came home to his wife with the great news from the doctors that he was now fully recovered.

"I can start going into work a few days a week. I can play nine holes of golf. I can even have sex three times a week."

"That's wonderful, darling," said his wife. *"Put me down for one, will you?"*

QUESTIONS

1. How good a sex life would you say you have now?

2. Can any difference of view on sex between you and your partner be easily solved?

3. Does the thought of dating again make you feel you'd prefer to swim the Channel?

CHAPTER 12

"The secret of staying young is to live honestly, eat slowly, and lie about your age."

Lucille Ball

You Are as Young as You Look

Does your appearance matter? Yes, it does

Old attitudes die slowly, and I suspect that, in spite of October 2006, to look 'old' will continue to be a disadvantage in some work places for a while. If you feel that might be true in your situation, then that leaves you with a decision to make.

Do you let your appearance stay as it is, somewhat changed perhaps by decades of hard work and dissolute living? Or do you do something about it? And, if you decide the latter, how far do you go?

To those of you who might be thinking that this is all a bit trivial, I suggest that it is in fact a very important decision, relevant to anyone who wants to combine work and play in their Third Act.

This is my argument:

- The battle has started in the war against Ageism, but it would be very naive to expect it to be totally won this year or next, and some attitudes will linger on.

- Many of you, who intend to carry on working for many years, have to consider this prejudice. A recent management survey showed that 90% of senior executives feared that they would lose out if they looked too old, and that '*a youthful appearance is an important factor in professional success*'.

- People make instant judgements about others, based on little more than their appearance. This judgement is made within the first two minutes in nearly 90% of instances. So your appearance, not just your mind, needs to be right to pass the first hurdle. You may be young in heart and mind, but, if you look old, you may not be sending out that message. Therefore, you have to decide whether you need to check out your appearance.

- There is also a personal side to this. You may be content with the changed character you present, but your family may prefer you to go back to the 'you' they've always loved, and would welcome a little tampering with nature.

- Of course, you don't have to change. You can take the view that the world is going to have to take you the way you look, and, if they don't like it, too bad. You can tell yourself that you don't need their approval at work, and that, at home, your family and friends are quite happy to see you as you now are.

- Or, you can decide that you really did prefer yourself as you were for most of your life; that your appearance no longer reflects the real you; and that a younger appearance would certainly help in the work place.

- There seems to me to be nothing shameful, or unmanly, about caring for one's appearance. As we get older, from 40 onwards, our bodies often begin to show signs of wear and tear. Even those who have not abused their body with too much food or alcohol, or even too much sun, find it harder to keep that youthful look.

- Women know about this more than men. My wife has often said that she could never believe that God was a woman. "*If She had been, She wouldn't have made it so difficult for us to keep our looks.*"

- We, of course, are not so vain, but, as she pointed out to me, most men now use after-shave, colognes, shower gel, moisturiser, sun cream, deodorant spray, so what's the big deal?

One friend convinced me of the dramatic effect that can be brought without any great drama. Steven made three changes on the same day. He was 56 at the time, and decided that he needed to stop the decline in his appearance. He didn't like what he saw in the mirror, especially his mixed mousy/grey hair; his wife was now looking years younger than him; and he realised that he was looking a bit ancient compared to others in his team at work.

So he decided to do three things.

He started with his face and gave himself a natural tanned look, with a self-tanning cream. No more complicated than putting on a moisturiser after shaving, or rubbing your face with soap.

He then went to his hairdresser, and had his hair cut, restyled and coloured.

He had already had a preliminary test at the eye clinic, and he walked out of the hair salon and took a taxi to the eye surgeon. His wife met him there, and his eyes were lasiked in a quarter of the time it had taken the hairdresser to do his hair.

I met him that weekend, and there was a man who had lost the proverbial ten years. For him the miracle did work. He had lost his glasses, which had dominated his face. He had lost that mixture of grey and mouse hair that made him look slightly seedy. He had lost his pale face and looked twice as healthy.

He looked better, he felt better, and it inspired him to do what his wife had wanted him to do for years, which was to follow that day of change with a campaign to get fit.

He should, of course, have done that first, but, like most of us, he needed an extra incentive, and the change in his facial appearance was his incentive for the harder slog.

If you also take that decision to stop looking a stereotype oldie, then you have a choice of five changes, all of which can make a major contribution to your appearance.

- **Change the colour of your hair**. If you don't enjoy that stage when you have a mix of grey in your hair, a good hair colourist can change all that.

- **Change the colour of your face**. If you're not happy with the pale face you have, then the simple use of modern self-tans can give an instant, younger and healthier look.

- **Lose your glasses**, thanks to the magic of the laser.

- **Refind your body** by changing the way you eat and the amount of exercise you take.

- **Turn back the years with cosmetic surgery**.

Change your Hair Colour

If you're lucky enough to bypass grey and go straight to silver, then that's marvelous. A silver silhouette surrounding a tanned face can paradoxically look 10 years younger. For some girls, silver hair is even an aphrodisiac, especially if it's Mercedes silver and has a matching car and platinum card.

Equally, if you have dark hair, and greying temples suit you, then enjoy them. Unfortunately, for most of us, we get that half-way parting of mouse and grey, which simply looks scruffy and old. If you're unhappy with that look, then a good colourist can put colour back into your hair, with vegetable dyes, but without any drama.

Go to a good hairdresser, have your hair styled in the way that gives you a younger look, have it coloured with a vegetable dye, and walk out after a 100 minutes session, looking ten years younger. Before you leave the salon, ask them for a bottle of the magic elixir, so that you can redo your hair every month in the privacy of your bathroom.

A bad hair dye, or day, is a joke, but millions of men now go to a decent colourist from their 40s onwards, and no one else is aware of it.

For any man, who may feel uneasy about joining the Salon game, be assured of this. There's hardly a film star, business tycoon, or any of those glitterati in the social columns, who doesn't owe his more youthful appearance to some colourist somewhere.

Women have long known all about this game, and have learnt that it is a sensible idea to start de-greying as soon as the first signs of winter appear. This can easily happen in your late 40s, and, from then on, it becomes part of their monthly grooming service.

It's the same ritual for men. If you don t go straight to being a Silver Wolf, far better to keep your own colour over the decades than letting your hair go that messy mixture of mouse and grey.

Change your face colour

Trivial you may think, and you may be right. But the fact is that a tanned face looks healthier, and a healthy face looks younger. It doesn't transform you, but it helps, and most of us need all the help we can find.

Sadly, age has its signs that not even the fittest can hide. Our skins often go a sickly pallor if we work constantly indoors; we get broken veins, more smile lines than a London tube map, crows feet and finally those small brown spots.

Medals of age, according to some, but equally we may not have helped ourselves with smoking, drinking, and too much sun. Whatever the cause we don't need them. Women can hide some of them with careful make-up, but, thanks to the miracle of cosmetic technicians, all of us can now conceal the odd blemish with a fake tan.

We can now hide our medals of age under a self-tan that reeks of Riviera living, and simply gives us a tanned healthy look that does miracles for most appearances.

The great secret is never to put too much on, which can only make you look like a refugee from the local panto. Or, even worse, like some famous TV presenters we can all remember.

Start discreetly with the face and the back of your hands, and nowhere else.

It's no great deal, no different from putting on an after-shave lotion or a moisturiser, and it only needs doing once a week. All it does is to make you look healthier, younger and richer without leaving the bathroom.

This image was born in the 1930s, when some of the rich discovered the French Riviera as an amusing playground for their winters, and came back to their northern homes tanned from the Mediterranean sun.

Fifty years ago the rest of the world started burning itself on the beaches in an attempt to look glamorous. Sadly, we now know that the sun can be a killer, with skin cancer becoming the fastest-growing cancer in the country.

Fake tan has come good at the right time. It means we don't have to suffer those endlessly boring days lying on a beach like a sardine just to look healthy, and we don't have to risk getting skin cancer.

Lose your glasses

Instead of always losing your glasses, what I am suggesting is that you really could lose your glasses. After 50 years of age, nearly 90% of us need glasses for some purposes, and so they become a symbol of being old.

Of course, millions have to wear them at all ages, and they can look very attractive when carefully chosen to complement the face of a pretty 30-year old girl, but less so on us.

If you enjoy wearing glasses and use them as a dramatic prop at meetings, then by all means carry on with them. Just check that they actually suit your face and the image you mean to present. For a more permanent change, the miracle of laser technology has now made it possible for you to go without them for most of the time.

In 10 minutes the cornea of your eyes can be reshaped to give you back at least 90% of your eyesight. It is totally painless, and the effect is immediate. It is a miracle of modern technology, which was finally approved ten years ago in America, and over here is approved by Moorfields, who have their own clinic for this operation.

Lasik isn't some indulgence only for older people; it is for anyone who wants to be able to see without glasses. I have a ward, who had it done at 25, and howled her eyes out when she woke up at the clinic, looked out of the window, and saw birds flying for the first time in her life, without having glasses on her eyes.

Tiger Woods confessed to never actually seeing the golf ball clearly before having his eyes done – and now half of the world's top ten golfers have been lasiked. Hundreds of cricketers, athletes and tennis players have thrown away their contact lenses, and now have no fear of losing their sight in the locker room just before a match.

Being able to move without glasses, though, is rejuvenating for those of us who have lived through lenses for a lifetime. You certainly look younger; you probably feel younger; and you possibly begin to act younger.

This tiny operation is certainly worth a consultation. I am very happy with my lasik surgery, which I had done four years ago, and have added an appendix on this operation. *(See Appendix Three)*

Re-find your body

"*You can never be too rich or two thin*" is the famous quote of the Duchess of Windsor, which is palpable nonsense on both accounts, but it is true that the more overweight you are, the less healthy you are and the older you look.

It is also true that a fit body that is given some exercise and used sensibly not only makes you feel better, it makes you feel younger. Many an unfit body can look old at 50, feels old at 60, and starts collapsing at 70. Get back to the weight and shape you were for most of your life, and the change is dramatic.

As the Grand Plan for a happy Third Act only makes sense if you plan to be healthy as well as wise, it makes no sense to ask for health problems by having a body that it is not fit. If you don't get fit for yourself, do it for the family. If it doesn't seem that important for today, it certainly will be for tomorrow and all your tomorrows.

Most of us know that we eat too much, and so all we have to do is cut back on the amount. Most of us know that we don't exercise enough, and it isn't exactly rocket science to know that a half hour walk a day will make us feel and look better. *(See Chapter 10)*

Repair your face

This is the most dramatic change to be considered. Cosmetic surgery is still fairly rare for men in this country, but not among business tycoons, film stars, and Pop stars from our younger days.

Its promise is that it takes 10 years off your appearance, and it usually delivers that promise. I suspect that, in a few years, a face lift will become a fairly common operation, as prices fall and surgeons' skills rise. In America 1.3 million men had cosmetic treatment last year, and nearly 300,000 of them were over 55.

It is a dramatic act of vanity, of defiance against ageing, and an attempt to return to the way you looked not many years ago. The simple truth is that your face drops a couple of inches in those Second Act years from 25 to 55. The fallen skin produces jowls, narrowing eyes, double chins, and lines across the contour of your face.

Does it matter? Of course not – unless you regret the passing of the old you, or find the new 'dropped' you a hindrance in your work. The cost of this rebirth has now fallen to £2,000 in Europe, and takes only two weeks out of your life, before you can rejoin the world.

If you want to know more about this, I have gone into some detail in an appendix. *(Appendix Two)*

Whatever you decide to do about your appearance, one simple fact is unarguable. You are as young as you look: to yourself as well as other people. If you feel that you look old, then odds are that you will behave old, and only confirm the prejudice of ageism.

If you feel that you are still the same handsome fellow as you were 20 years ago, then you are more likely to behave as young as ever. That is why your appearance could contribute to the success of your Third Act, and that is why I suggest that it is a very important part of the Grand Plan.

QUESTIONS

1. Are you happy with your appearance?

2. If you made any changes, which would they be?

3. Would you consider lasik or cosmetic surgery?

CHAPTER 13

"Most men will die with prostate cancer, but not usually from it"

Tim Christmas

The Uniquely Male Problem

It is a myth that your Third Act is full of health problems, but one of them does need special attention

Most men are still only too unaware that there is a time bomb sitting between their legs, and it's not what you may have thought. It's the prostate. Women don't have one; it's our unique problem.

Few in the past knew it was there, what it does, and why anyone should be concerned. Even the great Leonardo da Vinci in his detailed anatomical drawings missed out just one gland. The prostate.

Today, prostate problems are slightly more discussed, but a recent Poll showed that seven out of ten men still don't know where it is, or what to do about any problems in that area.

I certainly didn't, when I had prostate problems in my early fifties, but was lucky enough to be treated in time by the famous London urologist, Tim Christmas, and fortunately it was non-cancerous. Very often, prostate problems are not cancerous, just an inflammation of the gland, or a bacterial infection, which has unpleasant effects, but not lethal.

But sometimes they are cancerous, and prostate cancer has become the biggest killer among male cancers. An estimated 10,000 men die every year from it, and nine out of ten men will have prostate problems at some time in their lives. Most are over 60, but the number of men with prostate problems in their early fifties has quadrupled in the last decade.

Sadly, in spite of the greater awareness of the damage that prostrate problems does to men's lives, it is still the Cinderella in the great palace of NHS health. The Government provides only £4 million for prostate research; but just over £12 million for breast cancer research.

The NHS still has no national prostate screening programme. No man over 50 can be denied a PSA test (which measures the level of our Prostate Specific Antigen), but many self-respecting doctors still don't ensure that their patients get it each year.

This then is the problem. Most of us know little about the prostate; and the NHS too often has little advice for men on how to reduce the possibility of getting prostate cancer. Nor how to recognise the symptoms, what the choices are of dealing with it, and what the unpleasant consequences of any operation might be.

The Prostate Problem

I suppose the reason for the lack of knowledge about the prostate from our side is that many are embarrassed to talk about it, even within the family. The prostate is part of our productive system and produces some of the fluid that produces semen. It's just under the bladder and so effects our water works.

The indications that all may not be well are usually in the bladder department. At best, it is having to get up several times a night to pee; at worst, it's a lack of control and a desperate rush to the loo. None of which exactly helps you to feel like the stud that you thought you were.

When you finally go to the doctor, and explain your problems, you may receive little help, except the advice to drink nothing after seven at night, but the good ones will send you for an immediate PSA blood test. There's a great deal of academic debate on just how good this test is, but it's the best we have for the moment.

As a rough generalisation, a reading under four should produce no panic, but anything over five suggests you might have a problem; if you're already going to the loo three times a night, you probably have. Any higher reading is taken very seriously, and your doctor will send you immediately to a urological specialist for tests.

For most of us, what happens next is an unamusing rectal examination, whereby various bits are plucked out of your prostate for biopsy. Then it's up to your consultant, who will review the results of the tests, and offer you a choice.

If cancer is detected, the urologist has a choice of treatments, which include Radiotherapy, Chemotherapy, Brachytherapy, Ice therapy, Hormonal therapy, and Gene therapy.

If there is no cancer revealed at that stage, he will probably discuss two scenarios with you. The first is what is discreetly called 'watchful waiting', known in investment circles as 'masterly inertia'. This can either mean your symptoms are not yet bad enough for surgery, or at your age it's not worth bothering. Ageism is often rife in prostate medicine.

The second is a Prostatectomy, which is the removal of the inside of your gland, and is neither easy to do nor pleasant to have. This operation is not simple, because the prostate is difficult to get at it and is surrounded by wiring. You lose a lot of blood, even when it's done by an experienced urological surgeon, and there aren't many of them in the UK.

They then do further biopsies on samples from the wall of your prostate to check for cancer. If you're lucky, you are then clear, but, even if there is no cancer, the removal of the prostate can have some serious results.

Impotence does not boost anyone's confidence; lack of some bladder control does not enhance the quality of life, nor does the more usual reverse ejaculation during sex.

10 Tips to Prevent Prostate Problems

Whatever the treatment, prostate problems can change your life, and are best avoided, or at least postponed. The things that you can do to reduce the risk of your getting prostate cancer all come with the caveat that the medical profession isn't totally certain why you get it, and therefore how you can stop it.

None of the following are guaranteed to prevent prostate problems, but all of them have some sound research evidence to show that they slow the symptoms from coming, and alleviate them when they do come.

1. **Eat tomatoes**. They are rich in the chemical lycopene, which is the most abundant carotenoid in the prostate gland. Have tomatoes or a tomato sauce (not ketchup which has little tomato) at least 10 times a week, and you could reduce the possibility of your getting cancer by 45%. If you can't take them fresh, use pills like Lycomato, which contain concentrated extract.

2. **Take saw palmetto**. This berry counteracts the effects of reduced testosterone (which explains why the Red Indians used it as a mild aphrodisiac), and reduces inflammation of the enlarged prostate, thus allowing greater urine flow. There's a case for starting this as a daily drug from 50 onwards, to help prevent the nocturnal visits.

3. **Drink green tea**. Green tea takes some liking, but its phytochemicals seem to do wonderful things to the prostate. In China, where green tea is taken every day, only 2% of the men have prostate cancer; in America, where they rarely sip green tea, it is 55%. Not a true comparison, of course, but it might be significant.

4. **Prenez Pygeum**. In France, over 80% of all prescriptions for benign prostate problems are for Pygeum. There is evidence to show that it reduces any enlargement in two out of three cases.

5. **Eat a lot of broccoli**. This is the wonder vegetable that can do more for us than all the others.

6. **Take a twice weekly meal of oily fish**. The omega 3 oils have a beneficial effect; few Eskimo men have prostate problems.

7. **Stop smoking**. Heavy smokers are four times more likely to have prostate problems.

8. **Lose weight**. Overweight men are twice as likely to have prostate problems. Get back to your correct weight, walk at least half an hour every day, and your prostate is more likely to stay healthy.

9. **Note any change in your water works**. The earlier a prostate problem can be treated, the greater hope of a routine cure.

10. **Check your PSA every year**. Your doctor may not remember, but put it in your diary, and insist on the blood test every year.

Which 'magic' ingredient works best for you may never be clear, but it's worth remembering the summing-up one specialist told me:

"You're most likely to get prostate problems if you're over 50, have a family history of prostate problems, smoke 20 cigarettes a day, are two stone overweight, and eat a diet heavy in meat and dairy products. But eat and drink sensibly, and you can help yourself to beat it."

By the way, don't think it's just an older man's problem. The average age is still in the early sixties, but now it's coming down to the fifties, and even the late forties. According to some medical evidence, a third of us have already developed problems in the prostate by the time we're 55.

Prostate problems are a serious danger to all men, but we need to get it into proportion. For most, it doesn't even need an operation; for those of us who do have to have one, the problems can usually be cured. It will become even less of a danger, if you follow the ten tips, and, above all, get your PSA blood test done every year.

Excellent information is put out by several Prostate Cancer charities. *(See Appendix 4)* For the moment, I pass on what my surgeon told me. Most of us will die *with* prostate cancer, but not *from* it.

QUESTIONS

1. Do you need to change any part of your lifestyle to avoid this male problem?

2. Do you know your PSA?

3. Have you begun to notice any changes in your water works?

CHAPTER 14

"You're never too old to dream a new dream, but they become dearer each year."

Noel Coward

Do You Need More Pension Plans?

Probably yes, but how?

Most of us, in the previous 30 years, had a choice of two kinds of pensions, two ways that we could invest for our Third Act. If we worked for a large company with a good employees scheme, then that was the better route. If we didn't and had to make our own plans, then we were probably sold a Personal Pension policy, to mature at sometime from 55 onwards.

The company scheme would be subsidised by our employer; the personal plan by the government. Whatever we put into the company scheme, the company would at least match and often exceed. If we stayed with the company we would, at the end, receive a pension based on a percentage of our final salary.

To persuade us to save privately for our Third Act, the government contributed to any personal pension plan that we took out, to the amount of our tax bracket. If we paid tax at 40%, then for every £1000 we wanted to invest, the government would pay £400.

Of course, you know that, but I thought it worth a reminder of why we went into those plans, which meant that we put all our money for later years into the stock market. We knew that the government of neither Party was going to give us a decent pension, and so we had to plan our own.

Unfortunately, both those schemes now have problems. Taking the private alternative first, as anyone who has closed their pension plan in the last few years knows, it hasn't produced the value or the annuity expected.

As an example I give you a colleague's story. He had paid, every month for 30 years, into a policy that was expected to bring him, he was told in writing, a fund worth around a million pounds. At an annuity rate of 14%, and after taking out £250,000 in cash, he should be able to expect slightly over an annual income of £100,000.

When the time came to take the policy last year, he was told that it was, in fact, worth only £725, 000. After taking out £180,000, he would have £545,000 to buy an annuity. The best rate in the market that he could find was 6%, which gave him an annual income of just over £32,000. After tax this came down to £26,000 a year. He's not going to starve, but it doesn't seem a fortune after 30 years of investment.

As for the company pension schemes, the future of these was thrown into further confusion, when Rentokil became the first FT100 to close the final salary scheme, not just to new, but also to existing staff. By the beginning of 2006 it was estimated that the pensions deficit across all the companies in the FT100 alone exceeded £75 billion, and that over 90% have a pension deficit.

At the same time, the government announced that it was short by £60 billion to meet its own current pension commitments. Suddenly, they told us, pensions were in crisis.

Is There Really a Pension Crisis?

Yes, there is. Not yet as big as the government would have you believe, but there are serious problems. If these fail to improve, then we will have a real crisis before the decade is out. All three pension areas are in trouble. The government has committed itself to paying pensions to its public sector staff of a greater size and at a younger age than in the private sector, and now has a future liability well in excess of £500 billion. 90% of major company pension schemes are in deficit; and our personal pension plans are not producing the sums anticipated. Each of us has a problem.

The 10 factors that have contributed to the financial challenge of your Third Act include these:

- **Most of us have not saved enough in the last 30 years** for the Third Act, when we will be earning less. We all knew how much we should have saved, if we wanted to have a modest pension of half our gross earnings available from 65, but we didn't.

  We knew about the birthday rule; that, at whatever age you start, the percentage of earnings that you should then pay in to a pension policy is half your age. At 30, we should pay in 15%; at 40 years old, 20%; and at 50, 25% a year, all until we reach 65.

  In fact, only a few of us ever did pay anywhere near the required amount in any decade. Which inevitably means that most of us are not likely to have as much pension as we need.

- **We are going to live longer, and any pensions or investments that you have organised will have to cover more years than expected**. As most of us are going to live at least into our late seventies, and many of us into our eighties, then we will obviously need more pension money each year, just to stand still. Even those who have invested well in pension plans will find that their annuities are not going to increase enough for them to keep up with inflation for 20 and more years.

- **In the Eighties and Nineties companies threw out older people**. Companies cut their costs by sending millions into early retirement, and the government were forced to pick up the bill. This stupid act of ageism, now finally illegal, has left the government with an annual bill of £30 billion, as well as forcing millions out of useful work.

  With the anti-ageism legislation of October 2006, companies will no longer add to this sum, and hopefully will be able to use the experience of many presently out of work. But it has added to government social security costs.

- **Pension funds have not produced the results promised**. The fund managers blame the stock market, for their poor performance, but many put it down just as much to poor management and high fees. It is true that the equity market has scarcely risen over the last decade, while bond rates have fallen, but presumably the reason we pay high fees is for investment management skills in bad times.

  Whatever the cause, the result is that the anticipated value of most funds has not been met. Final values may be improved when the market value of the shares in the portfolio rises, but annuity rates are not likely to rise.

- **Company pension funds have a total deficit of at least £130 billion**, owing to the taking of pension holidays and reduced annual payments. Nearly half of the FT100 companies have closed their final salary or defined benefit schemes to new staff. The worry now is whether your scheme can survive in its original form, or whether the final salary version will soon be replaced by a lower pension based on average earnings.

  Two things are certain. Companies will have to allocate far more funds into their pension schemes, and some have already begun to do this. It is also clear that your individual contribution will have to increase, as part of trying to bring the scheme back to some equilibrium. And your final salary scheme could easily disappear overnight.

  What is less certain is what the market needs to do to increase the value of the fund. It has been claimed that a 25% growth would almost solve the whole crisis. In other words, once the FT100 rises above the 7000 figure that it reached at its peak, then much of the company and personal pensions crisis could be reduced.

  But, even so, to solve the total deficit will require more than a raging stock market; it will need far more efficient handling of your pension money, and that is not guaranteed.

- **The Government never set up a State Pension Fund**. All that money, which we pay in each year as part of the National Insurance contribution, goes into one giant Treasury pot. So, there is no separate Pension Fund, in which our pensions have been earning compound interest over decades.

  This is the mother of all swindles, and it is beyond comprehension why successive governments have not rectified this fundamental mistake. This is a major contributor to any pension crisis.

- **Governments have not increased the State pension in line with earnings for over 20 years**. Margaret Thatcher changed the state pension to follow costs, not earnings, an act of gross meanness. If she hadn't made that change, the current pension would be 50% higher. The Socialists, once the party of the people, have not changed it, even though it has been in power since 1997.

- **Governments have messed around with the state pension system seven times in the last 25 years, and got it wrong every time**. They brought in SERPS, MIG, second state pension, pension credits, equalising ages, and the stakeholder pensions. They confused it further by a social security bundle that is incomprehensible even to the workers in their offices. They continue to meddle and even change packages before they come into operation, as they did with the so-called revolutionary simplifying of pensions in May 2006.

  They have so messed up the pension situation that the UK pension is now 26th lowest among the 30 countries analysed by the OECD. The average across all OECD countries is 69% of pre-retirement income; in the UK it is 48%.

- **Gordon Brown has removed billions from the private pension funds** ever since 1998, when he withdrew the tax exemption on dividends paid to pension funds and charities. Some claim that the total figure removed by 2006 has exceeded £60 billion. Whichever amount it is, it has increased the dangers of a real pension crisis, not only because it reduces the value of our pensions, but also our individual trust in any savings scheme.

- **There are too many government employees**. The current government have employed too many people on far too generous pension terms. Unbelievably 80% of government employees have guaranteed final salary schemes, against only 15% in the private sector, some two million. They are also allowed to take these from 50 onwards. This is the real source of the state pension crisis.

Clearly these generous terms cannot continue. The government claims it can not afford to pay these pensions that it has promised.

B rought together, all these factors in the pension equation have lead to a crisis, which will grow throughout this decade. It is one that can partly be solved by a growth in stock market prices, and particularly from larger contributions by companies. But, even more importantly, it needs clear action by the government to make tax changes that would prevent a problem becoming a crisis.

In the event that they fail to act quickly, what will you do with your pension plans now? When you have done your figures for your Grand Plan (*see Chapter 7*), and find that you will need an extra source of income ten or more years down the line, how will you achieve that?

Is it now worth taking out a new pension in your fifties, adding more to your existing one, or moving your money elsewhere? And if so, how?

As always in your Third Act you are the only one who can make the best decisions for you, but you have at least seven alternative actions.

Seven Choices of Action on Your Pension

1. **You can change nothing**. If you have a company scheme, you continue to contribute, even though it will become an increased contribution. If you have a personal pension plan you continue to pay the same every month. This may prove to be what some investors call 'masterly inertia', and others call 'playing ostrich'.

2. **You can cease paying into your personal plan, and make it paid up**. You can hope that the value will grow with the stock market over the next decade, but you are not prepared to add further moneys to your plan. By ceasing to make further contributions, you leave your pension fund to grow, but retain your monthly contributions to use in a different way.

3. **You can end your personal plan altogether**, take your 25% cash now to invest in another project, and buy an instant annuity or start a draw down plan. You thus save your monthly contributions, and acquire both fresh capital and income. Or you can now take the 25% tax-free cash, but leave the remainder to continue as a pension policy. The May 2006 changes allow you to continue working, but also take a contribution from your pension.

4. **You can increase the payments into your personal plan**, in the belief that the stock market will boom, and you will take advantage of the government 40% subsidy to build up a larger sum. The revised pension rules from May 2006 allowed you to pay far more of your earnings into a plan. For high earners the annual contribution allowance has risen to £215,000.

    If you do decide to continue with the managed personal pension fund route, there are three points worth remembering, and which may not have been pointed out to you by the salesman many years ago.

- **It is worth checking on the performance of your fund managers**. Fund managers have different approaches to investment, but what most of them have in common is a poor track record.

    Their skills in all kinds of markets have rarely produced the expected results. Only one in ten of all managed funds beats the FT100 index, which means that only one in ten does better than your putting your money into a Tracker Fund.

    Fund managers, as has been noted earlier, currently blame the UK stock market for being no higher in 2006 than it was in 1997. But there have been plenty of good times in the last 30 years, and an especially fast growth in 2004–6. Even so, in both bull and bear markets, most of them have failed to beat the index.

    Markets have boomed all over the world, and yet the pension fund managers have still produced a meagre return, often because they are restricted as to where they may invest. Did they tell you that, when you started to give them your monthly money?

    If you decide to continue with them, find out what restrictions they have on where they can invest. The UK market has performed badly in comparison with other markets for a long time, and you don't want your money stuck only in one marketplace.

- **It is worth checking on their costs**. Their failures come at a high price. Their charges are not kept secret, but few of us realise just how high they add up. Out of your 30 years of contributions into your personal pension plan, they can easily have taken some 30% in implicit and explicit costs. Many cost less than this, but does yours?

    These costs include the percentage charged on your initial units each year until you close the pension, the further percentage for management fees taken off each and every further contribution, annual charges, and a mixture of dealing and administrative fees.

    At a time when returns are at a historical low, their costs can absorb almost half of your growth. Some analysts believe that the average net return in recent years on many pension funds is under 2%, after all costs. Ask the organisation, which sold you your plan, to check out the percentage of money that you are losing on your contributions.

- **It is important to remind yourself that the pension fund money is never totally yours**. If you are going to take out a new pension in your Third Act, the government subsidy would, as before, obviously save you a lot of money. If you plan to put in £10,000 a year over the next 10 years, this will cost you £100,000, if it goes into some scheme of your own. Yet it would cost only £60,000 if you take the government subsidy and join a new pension plan.

  But the downsides of the government subsidy pension plan are the restrictions when you end the policy. What is sometimes forgotten is that you are only allowed to receive 25% of the value of your policy, and you have to buy an annuity with the remainder. You may then be restricted by a low return for the rest of your life, and neither you nor your family will ever have sight of the main capital.

5. **You can increase your payments into the company plan**, in the belief that companies will quickly top up their schemes, and that a dramatic upswing in the stock market will reduce any panic among fund trustees. Company pensions are never likely to be as generous in the future as they were ten years ago, but they are still the best deal going.

6. **You can personally invest for the future without company or government subsidy**. This is an alternative for you, if you prefer to have total control over your investments, and wish to ensure that the total investment reverts to you at the end, rather than remaining with an insurance company

   A Tracker Fund inside an Isa is an obvious example of the route some have taken with a small part of their funds. These follow the stock market, but you pay no large management costs, no tax on the profits, and receive all your money when you cash in.

This is a brave approach, but, if your £10,000 a year could be invested in such a way as to produce over 5% a year growth, it could soon cancel out the loss of the government pension fund subsidy, if only because of the reduced costs. It also leaves you free to do with your final money as you wish, instead of losing it to the insurance company.

7. **You can consider investing in property**. If you have little confidence in the stock market, and decide to end further contributions to any fund managers, take a look at the possibilities with property.

The property market has risen at much the same rate as the stock market in the last 50 years, and has the benefit of being geared. You may want to invest in a second home in the sun (*see Chapter 19*), or you may opt to become a landlord and join the Buy to Let investors. Many see this an alternative pension plan to come to fruition 10–15 years down the line, and which, in price-rising times, can be the basis of a heavily geared business (*see Chapter 17*).

What you decide to do obviously depends on your situation, which will be affected by your age, your investments and whatever shortfall you have identified. The only thing common to 90% of us is that we have to take some action.

As we have seen in other pages of *Silver Wolf*, even today's low inflation rate means that we will need twice the income we have now, if we hope to continue living at the same standard in 25 years.

On top of that your pension income is probably going to be far less than expected; and you are going to live longer than you expected 30 years ago.

It inevitably follows that at the beginning of your Third Act you need to have a clear picture of what any of your existing policies may bring, and how much more you need to invest now, while there is still time for the investment to grow,

You have seen that the State pension is only a gesture, and is unlikely to grow significantly. You will know that your Company pension may well be less than expected, if final salary schemes are ended.

Your personal pension plan has been reduced by three factors not under your control – the removal by the Chancellor of £5 billion a year, the collapse of the stock market and the arrival of an era of low inflation.

If there is a real crisis to come, then it will be, as usual, largely the fault of governments. They need to promote better fiscal incentives to all of us to save at every point of our lives, and then add more incentives to work for as long as we want to, without our being penalised by taxes that have no part in the new Third Act society.

Government has already begun to take the action needed to deal with the changing demographics, but should now seize the initiative given by the 2006 Age Discrimination Act to change nearly all the rules of the game. With a few radical changes, millions more will be able to save more efficiently, work part time until they wish to stop, and continue to contribute fully to the economy.

That way, there may well not be as large a Pension Crisis as the Government currently warns, and, by the action that you decide to take today, you will be able to ensure enough funds to enjoy all the years of your Third Act.

QUESTIONS

1. Do you need to change any of your pension plans now?

2. Are you tempted to leave the stock market and invest in property?

3. How much more income will you need in 10 years?

Getting the Most Money for Your Annuity

Even if you don't take out any more pension plans at this time, but simply continue with the existing ones, when you do finally take money from any of your personal pension, you have a set of new decisions to make.

1. When you know the value of your pension fund, you have the option to take 25% of in tax-free cash. You don't have to take it, but you should. It's the last bit of your pension that won't be taxed.

2. The rest of your money has to be used in one of three ways. The usual is to buy an annuity immediately, but, if your pension pot is substantial, you can also choose between a phased retirement and an income drawdown. Both have disadvantages, but they give greater flexibility and are worth exploring.

3. This is far too important a decision to decide without advice, and you should use an investment advisor who has experience in this market, like *Dennehy Weller* or *Hargreaves Lansdown;* or specialist companies, like the *Annuity Bureau* or *Annuity Direct*, who only deal in annuities.

4. Don't forget that annuities are a one-time buy and you can't change; you only have the one chance to use your fund money.

5. You can delay your annuity purchase for years, but it's rarely worth it. Annuity rates don't look like rising, and, even with a two year delay, it could take 15 years to recoup the income you lost in those two years. Annuity prices have been falling for 16 years, and long gone are the days of double digit annuities.

6. Remember that you don't have to accept what your own pension fund is offering you for an annuity. You have an Open Market option to buy from any provider who is offering the best deal. So, once you know your valuation,

offer it on the open market. The difference between the best and the worst offers is often 25% for every year of the rest of your life. Sadly in the past, two out of three people have not bothered to look around, and have bought the annuity offered by their pension company.

7. The final annual amount offered to you by the insurance companies depends much on your age and the variation of annuity that you choose, but illness is another factor. Don't forget that if you still have any bad habits, this is when you benefit. If you've smoked for 10 years and are overweight, the actuaries reckon you won't live as long and offer you more now. Best thing is to take their 'sick' offer and give up next day!

8. There are half a dozen variations of annuities, with further options within some of them, and you need to be clear as to what guarantees you want. You can choose from an annuity that is level, escalating, investment linked, with profits, with wife, with guaranteed length of time, flexible, and so on. Get all the sums for each choice, and work out your best answer with your advisors.

9. At today's low rates, their lowest for 40 years, this may not seem the best time to take out an annuity, but don't pity yourself too much. In relation to the cost of living they are high. Annuities are now double the rate of inflation, whereas, when they were over 10% ten years ago, the cost of living was often higher.

10. If you're in no desperate hurry to cash in your pension, it's worth noting that some companies change their final bonus calculation each month. As circumstances change, so does the bonus, and your advisers can alert you to any special offer. A half per cent may not sound much, but over 20 or more years it becomes significant.

11. The final insult is that your annuity money will then have to be declared and taxed. The government's attitude is that they gave you a tax perk of 22 or 40%, when you paid in your premiums, and now they would like it back, precisely at the time when you need the income most.

CHAPTER 15

"A house is more than a home; in times of need it is a man's best friend."

George Bernard Shaw

Need More Money?

No problem. Get it out of your property

It has never been easier to raise money from your home. It doesn't matter what you need money for, it can be found. Which is a great relief to most of us, who, at some stage in our Third Act, are probably going to need some extra cash.

You may need it to achieve one of your leisure ambitions in the Grand Plan. Enjoying a month in a painting school in Provence; taking a scuba diving course in the Red Sea; getting your pilot's license in Florida; or joining Prince Charles meditating in a monastery.

Maybe you want to ride your horse along the old cowboy routes across the USA; spend a winter in Florence writing your memoirs; or play the great courses of the world in an annual golf tour. Or you need it to buy that home in the sun.

More prosaically, you may simply come to need it to keep up the quality of life that you want to enjoy. The reality of life is that, however much we may plan to balance the budgets, rising costs mean that we need more money every year, just to stand still.

Inflation, even as low as it is today at, say, 3%, still means that our costs will double in 24 years. A way of life that only needs £25,000 at 55 years will need around £38,000 at 70 and around £50,000 by 80.

Whatever the reason for wanting more money, it's in the home that you have one of the best means to supply it. Most of us are fortunate enough to have property that has leapt in price every decade, and gives us some collateral for a loan.

Many in the lending fraternity still like to see their normal mortgages paid off by the time you're 70, but there are now several ways to release cash from your home at any stage in your Third Act.

To decide which way is best for you needs a lot of personal discussions and decisions. You have to be honest about the way you see your lives over the next decades, and you need to lay down your priorities. It may be the last major financial decision you take, and is certainly one of the most important.

Basically you have a choice of five main ways to free some capital from the house, and each of them affects your future life style:

1. **Sell up and move to a cheaper home**
2. **Sell up and rent any future home**
3. **Borrow from the bank**
4. **Take a mortgage that doesn't need servicing**
5. **Take an interest/only mortgage**

Sell the house and move to a cheaper home

This is the easiest way of raising some money, and it's what most financial advisers recommend. The advantages are obvious:

- You sell your home for, say, £400,000, and buy a smaller version for £250,000, thus freeing £150k. You still have a home, but now have more capital to enjoy your Grand Plan.

- You have no loans to service, and running costs of the new home are normally lower.

But there are also disadvantages to consider:

- Moving costs can easily swallow up £20,000.

- Moving home – and particularly downsizing – is traumatic, second only to divorce.

Your decision on this choice depends on so many factors. *(See Chapter 6)* You may agree with the financial advisers that this is the most sensible way to raise cash, but is it right for the life that you have mapped out in your Grand Plan? Only you can give those answers.

Sell the house and rent

Selling your home and *not* replacing it brings in the maximum mount of capital without debt. You sell for £400,000, and perhaps keep only your favourite pieces of furniture. You then rent somewhere else for £10,000 upwards a year. The advantages are obvious:

- You keep *all* the money from the house sale.

- You can invest it all, drawing down sums whenever you need them.

- You no longer have home running costs, and can leave maintenance worries to your various landlords.

- You are free to move at any whim, and so can live for months or years in different parts of the country and throughout the world.

More and more people are taking this route, because of the freedom it brings. It means that one single home is no longer important to you; you make a new home every time you move. But it has one financial downside, and one psychological.

- Would you be happy without a home of your own? Is a home wherever you put your head down, or is it the place which you made, and where you are surrounded by your belongings?

- Are you prepared to opt out of the property market, which has proved to be the best single investment in the UK market in the last 50 years, and which could double your capital in the next decade?

- Without a home of your own, you lose the collateral for any future loan that might be needed.

This doesn't mean, of course, that you can't sell now, rent, and then buy later, after a few years of freedom. That can work wonderfully if you get the house market right and sell near the top, and then buy again near the bottom. Not so clever an idea if you make the wrong judgement.

Borrow from the Bank

Your bank can help you to raise capital, but this route only makes sense these days if you have a good relationship with your bank manager, and he/she is prepared to grant you a loan against your house, and at a decent rate.

It won't be a large loan, probably 15–20% of the value of the property, and the bank will need to be certain that you can afford the monthly servicing of the loan.

Now that the building societies have entered the Third Act mortgage market, there is less reason to go to the bank. The bank interest rate is often dearer than the building society, and the up-front costs usually greater, with arrangement, legal and completion fees.

On the other hand, if you prefer to continue dealing with someone you know, then this way could be the answer, especially if you are not seeking a very large sum.

Take out an Equity Release Plan

This is now a booming market, and it is easy to see why. In simple terms, an equity release lifetime mortgage allows you to borrow money based on the value of your house. It is not dependent on your income; nor do you ever have to repay any interest or capital.

- What this mortgage offers is a lump sum or a borrowing facility, untaxed, and with no obligatory repayments of capital or interest until the house is sold. You simply forget about the plan.

- You can use it for any purpose you choose, from buying a home in the sun to paying off the credit cards.

- You can borrow between 18% and 40% of the value of the property, with the exact percentage depending on your age when you take it out. Many of the providers of these plans start with offering 20% at 60, and then allow one per cent more with each year. So at 70 they will lend 30%, and 40% at 80.

- You retain 100% ownership of your property; and you benefit from any increase in the value. If you need more money later, the Lender will consider granting more, because of both your greater age and any greater value of the property.

- You can never be thrown out, even if the property market collapsed and the value of your home fell to less than the amount you own.

- You can move the deal to another property, so long as the new value covers the existing loan, or pay it back when you sell.

Sounds too good to be true? No, it is true, but, as always, there are downside factors and you must choose carefully which provider you take.

- The first downside is the amount of interest the Lenders charge for this service. Because they're not going to get any money back until you die, they often charge more than they would for a normal mortgage. At the time of going to press, for example, this varies from 6.0–8.0%, rather than the lower mortgage rate of 4.5–6.5%.

- Because of this higher interest rate, the second downside is even stronger. In return for the concession that you do not pay interest at any time in your life, they roll up the interest each day, so that each day you are not only incurring interest on the sum you borrowed, but also interest on each day's accumulated interest.

- What this means is that, if you take out an equity release plan at a rate, say, of 7%, your debt doubles in 10 years. Borrow £100,000 today, and in 10 years you will owe £202,000. In 16 years you will owe £306,000.

- The up-front charges are not small. They differ from one Lender to the next, but you will have a fee for valuation, for the lawyer, for the application, for the arrangement and may find yourself £2,000 down to start with.

I was sceptical about these plans in the past, but I now believe they will change the lives of millions, who find they need more money to fulfil their dreams. Home reversion is a different scheme and not one I would recommend, but lifetime mortgages for the later years could change your life. Whether they are right for you depends on your financial situation, your age, and your family.

- It is perfect for the SKI Club, the Spend the Kids Inheritance brigade. If you take the decision that the kids are going to be fine, and that you are going to use all your money to make your Third Act as enjoyable as you can, then you won't care if the compound interest bill takes a large chunk of the house sale. You have your money, and you keep your home.
    You simply borrow the maximum allowed, and then top it up when the house has increased its value. You have to pay

nothing out every month, and the bill is only finally met when your paraglider comes down in the ocean.

- It is the only plan for those who need money, and do not want to sell, but do not have enough guaranteed income to obtain a large mortgage or loan from the bank. With income irrelevant to this plan, large amounts can be borrowed simply against the value of the home.

- It is particularly relevant to those in their early seventies, who find they need more money to keep the Great Plan going, but who, according to the actuaries, will not usually be more than a decade accruing interest upon interest. Their loan will only have doubled in the decade.

- It can even be claimed to be tax efficient for owners of high value property, where the large final debt can be used to reduce the amount of Inheritance tax, but still leave a considerable sum to their children.

- It is most definitely not the best plan for anyone in their sixties. The compound interest factor really kicks in over long periods, and a £100,000 loan becomes a £400,000 debt after 20 years.

- It also makes less sense if you plan to move soon. Most plans are transferable, but at a cost, and, if you move to a much cheaper home, it may not be large enough to qualify for the same amount as your existing loan.

Flexible Loans

There is an interesting variation worth mentioning here, which makes even more sense. This is the Flexible Lifetime Mortgage, which has all the characteristics of a normal equity release plan, but has one great advantage. You organise a Borrowing Reserve with the Lenders, and only pay interest on the amount you have actually borrowed for immediate use.

You can, for example, arrange a Flexible Life mortgage for

£100,000, and take only 20% of it immediately. This would then leave you with an £80,000 reserve facility, which you can draw down at any time in the following five or ten years.

After that, this borrowing facility ends, but by then, if the property market continues to rise, your increased age and the extra value will qualify you for another tranche.

The great advantage of this variation, of course, is that you are not paying rolled up interest on any moneys until you actually need to use them, and is therefore less costly than a normal release plan which charges interest on the whole loan from the first day.

This equity release market has grown from a few hundred thousand pounds at the Millennium to over one billion pounds by the end of 2005, when specialist advisers, like Key Retirement Solutions, reckoned that over 100,000 homeowners had borrowed over £5 billion in equity release mortgages. The average amount borrowed is just under £50,000.

It was a rather dodgy market in the Nineties, but it is well controlled now, and there is a mass of information supplied by law to anyone who applies for an Equity release plan. Help the Aged and Age Concern both have booklets on this scheme.

It is also an organised market, with its own trade association SHIP, Safe Home Income Plans, and genuine competition among Lenders. They differ over the rate of interest charged, over costs charged, and over the small print. It's very worthwhile finding the lowest interest rate, as even 1% makes a dramatic difference to the growth of the debt.

This is the last loan that most borrowers are likely to take, so follow the usual advice and compare hard, before deciding.

In particular, ensure that:

- the rate is the best in the market at the time
- you can move if necessary
- you can get a top-up when needed
- your interest rate cannot go up
- you still own 100% of the property

- you can take out your own house insurance
- your house will not have to be constantly revalued
- and you know exactly how much your costs are

If you are short of income, but want a large sum, these plans become worthy of serious consideration. Even if you still want to leave the family an inheritance, you can argue that, historically, your property will double again in the next ten years.

If that happens, there would still be enough for them after your compounded interest bill has been paid off. They would, of course, have to sell the house to repay the loan, unless they had had considerable spare capital.

If, on the other hand, you have the income, and can afford to service a loan, then the building societies offer an alternative, which will leave the family inheritance untouched.

Take out an Interest-Only Mortgage

Without any great publicity, some building societies have at last come to realise that we don't cease to be potential clients, just because we are over 45 +VAT. Nor do we cease to have an income that can give Lenders some collateral confidence.

Property is the main business of building societies, and, much to their credit, two of the most prestigious, Halifax and Nationwide, have pioneered the creation of Home Retirement Plans. These allow you to take out new mortgages at any age over 55, on the interest-only principle, and pay the interest monthly.

Like the equity release plans, these are also for life, usually fixed at 40 years, and the mortgage is repaid when you sell or die. The main difference from the mortgages that you probably had in earlier years is that you need never pay back the capital during your lifetime; you pay only the interest.

- Unlike equity release plans, your income now is the key to how much you can borrow. Your income includes all earnings, annuities, pension payments, interest from shareholdings, portfolios, etc. The building societies will happily lend you three times your income; sometimes four times, so that a loan of £100,000 normally requires a guaranteed income of £30,000.

If you require more, but lack sufficient income, then you may well be able to persuade the societies to accept guarantees from others in the family.

- With these plans you can borrow up to 65–75% of the value of the property. This means that, if you have the income, you can borrow far more than with an equity release plan.

- Very commendably, these societies do not use age to increase the interest rate. Currently, in 2006, it is around 5%, which is less even than some mortgages offered to first time buyers.

- But, and as always there is a but, this does have to be serviced on a normal basis every year. Currently that would cost £5000 for every £100,000 borrowed.

So who would find this version of a lifetime mortgage worth considering?

- It is ideal for those in their sixties, who have enough income to justify the amount of money they want to borrow, and can afford to service that loan. You get to keep your house. You get to keep any increase in value in the house. You get to stay with your friends and in the community where you are known.

- It is attractive to those who want to hand down to their children the maximum they can. By paying off the interest on the loan every month, there is only the capital to come off the inheritance. Your children get to inherit the property without any debts. In 15 years under this plan you will have paid back £75,000 in interest, and only the original £100,000 loan is left for the children to pay.

- It is right, if you want a larger sum than is available by equity release, but cannot bear to sell the house. Half the value of your house could be released, say, and then you can work out a way to service the interest payments, either alone or as a family.

- It is certainly not right for those struggling to pay basic expenses. Taking on the extra costs of a loan in these circumstances does no good to anyone.

Which plan is the best deal?

All these alternatives make it possible to use your home as collateral for a great deal of money. I believe that the Equity Release schemes will revolutionise the financial lives of many in the second half of their Third Act, just as the Building Society plans can change your life in the first half.

If you have the income, the building societies have the money at a commercial rate. If you have the property value, but not enough income, the equity release lenders have the money at a slightly higher rate.

Are there great financial differences between these alternatives? Take a look at how these schemes can work out in practice. Have a look at these three scenarios, based on someone with a £400,000 home, and aged 70, who would like to raise £120,000. The assumption is that each home doubles in value by the end of 10 years.

You'd expect there to be significant differences in the end results, but all is not quite as it first appears.

1. **Sell and buy something smaller**.
   At the age of 70, you sell your large home for £400k, and buy a smaller home for £280k after costs. You have no debt to service; you have the £120,000 to use, but you have a smaller home. Over the next 10 years the net £250,000 home doubles in value, following the historical pattern of doubling every

10 years. If you die at 80, your new home has then a value of £500k. You have had the £120k to use; nothing is owed on the house; your children inherit £500,000.

2. **Take out an Equity Release plan**.
   You do not sell the house, but get a lifetime equity release mortgage for £120,000 at 7%. You keep your old house, and have the £120,000 to use. You have no debt to service, because the interest is rolled over. Your home doubles in value to £800,000, but so does your debt, and you owe, after 10 years, £240,000. Your heirs inherit £560,000.

   At this point they inherit more than in option one, but this, of course, reduces with each extra year that you live into your eighties.

3. **Take out an Interest Only Mortgage**.
   You do not sell, but borrow £120,000 at 5% on a lifelong mortgage. You have the £120k to use. You have to pay interest of £6,000 every year. Your home doubles to £800,000; you owe £120k; and so your heirs inherit £680,000.

   This looks the best deal at first, but it ignores the reality that you have not had £120,000 to use. In fact, you only had £60,000, because of having to pay back interest of £60,000 at £6,000 a year.

   If you wanted to have the same amount of money to use throughout the ten years, then you would have to borrow far more. Or, of course, make an agreement with the family that they pay the interest charges in return for the higher inheritance.

One last thought. Don't forget the effect of CGT, if you're worried about how much you are leaving the children. Any inheritance over £300,000 attracts tax at 40%, so they will only actually receive some 60% of whatever you leave, above £300,000.

Only you can know which route is more comfortable for you, but the good news is that anyone in their Third Act can now free equity from their property in one way or another. Whether you do this by selling and downsizing, with an equity release scheme, or a home retirement plan will depend on your priorities and your resources.

QUESTIONS

1. If you wanted to raise money from your home, which way would work out best for you?

2. If you were to sell your home, would you use money to buy a smaller home in UK and one in the sun? Or, would you want to have no UK residence, but live round the world in rented homes?

3. What is your attitude to leaving money for your children?

CHAPTER 16

"No man is so rich that he can pass a £50 note on the pavement without picking it up."
Nubar Gulbenkian

Cut Your Costs

You've done a fitness and appearance audit, now save thousands in a financial audit

This could seem a rather boring chapter about taking care of the routine daily costs of living. What makes it interesting is that you could save several thousands of pounds just for a few days work.

What I'm suggesting is that you do a Financial Audit on your domestic costs. This could save you thousands in the first years and hundreds in subsequent years. Act like a Financial Comptroller would in any business, see where money is being wasted, and make the changes needed.

Inertia combined with laziness usually means that we give less attention to our personal costs than we do to our company costs. That's why I've tried to bring together here a collection of thoughts that might help. Some of them have been mentioned in greater detail in other chapters, but I've included them here as a reminder.

Nothing is more tedious than worrying about every detail of your money, and I'm not suggesting that, but the less money we waste, the more we have to fulfil the Great Plan. What I am suggesting is that you run a check over your suppliers and switch where you find a better deal.

All it takes is a few days. Prepare a list of all your services you are paying for, and what they are costing you. Then get out the relevant bills that will give you all the information that anyone will need if you want to switch to them. When you're ready, go on the web, or the telephone, and start dealing. Cancel any old bad deals and renegotiate the rest.

1. THE MORTGAGE

If you still have a mortgage on any of your homes, it's worth checking if you are getting the best deal. Long gone are the days when it was best to stick with your existing mortgage lender.

There are three good reasons to change. First, the Lenders want new clients and so they are wooing you to switch to them. Second, there is no such thing as loyalty any more; it's the new client who is offered the best deals. Thirdly, it's now easy to switch, and costs very little.

Switching mortgage lenders can literally save thousands from a few hours checking the net, giving the problem to a broker, or taking a stroll down the High Street.

It's the same with remortgages. If your existing Lender doesn't offer what you want, other building societies are queuing to help you. Many sites on the web, such as *moneysupermarket.com*, will show you all the offers available.

We changed lenders for a remortgage and saved £1,300 a year on the original quote.

2. LIGHT & HEAT

This is another very competitive market, with dozens of suppliers wanting your business. Most of them cover both gas and electricity, and so can supply both services. They also take care of the paperwork. It's worth asking for quotes on gas and electricity separately, as these are often cheaper than buying both from the same supplier.

Several web sites will compare services, once you give them where you live and the amount of power you usually use. I check with *uSwitch.co.uk*, but there are others. We're only talking a few hundred pounds saving here, but the first time I checked, we did save £350 in twenty minutes. With energy bills increasing annually the family fuel bill is now a serious sum.

3. INSURANCE

- **Home insurance**
  For some reason, insurance companies think you're a better bet after 50 and their premiums drop. You will probably want some cover on the house, but the premiums are still high, with endless small print that you only discover too late.

  Most insurers make serious profits on their home insurance premiums, so check around on the web; and have a look at the actual policy before you sign. The difference in premiums can be enormous, with some over twice as high as others for the same contract.

- **Travel insurance**
  Not an enormous sum, but travel agents charge far too much for this insurance. Never buy from them, nor is it worth buying for every journey. Take out an annual policy, which is often less than the fortnight's policy that the travel agent tries to sell you. If your insurance broker doesn't know this market, google in *travel insurance* on the web for pages of choices.

- **Motor insurance**
  Rates often get lower as you get older, as, once again, the insurers seem to think that anyone over 50 is a better risk. Loyalty means nothing here, so each year you are better to take your No Clams Bonus with you and request quotes from other companies. Most companies will often quote a cheaper rate to a new prospect than for a renewal for an existing one.

  Best deals here are obtainable on the telephone, and half an hour of calls can make a difference of several hundred pounds. If you would really prefer to stay with your existing company, find out what others would charge you, then go back to yours and give them the price that they have to match, if they want to keep you. They usually will.

- **Health insurance**
  Now, this is serious money, and, as Clint Eastwood once famously asked, *"Well, punk, do you feel lucky?"* The same applies to you and medical insurance. You have to take a gamble on whether health insurance is still worth the money, and therefore worth continuing, as it becomes dearer and dearer, with every age milestone you pass.

  You'll find that premiums rise quickly from 60, because the actuaries have got their figures wrong. They reckon we are likely to have a lot of illnesses in the next 20 years, and so charge high premiums. In fact, statistically, most of us are unlikely to have much more illness than in previous decades, so you might think that £3–6,000 a year could be better kept, as you move through your years.

  It's worth noting that, among those with private health plans, only one person in 25 ever makes claims over £5,000 a year.

  Personally, we decided to set up our own private health fund, investing into it each year the same amount of money as the premiums would cost. That way we have it for use against the day when one of us might need medical help quicker than was possible under the NHS. If nothing happens, then we get to keep the money. Our first £10,000 went into premium bonds as a quickly releasable gamble.

  But, if you feel unlucky, then you might prefer to carry on your insurance. With heart bypasses at £15,000 and prostate operations at £5,000, private attention can hurt your bank account as much as your body.

  If you want some cover for less premiums, you could check out organisations like *Health Now*. Also look at the companies like *Exeter* that do not automatically put up your premiums, as you grow older each year.

- **Payment Protection insurance**
  This product is the joy of the insurance industry. It's been estimated that we give them over £5billion of premiums a year for this policy, which they sell us to cover payment of our financial commitments.

The reality is that this policy is often as porous as a sieve, and full of let-out clauses – like being over a certain age – which might explain why less than 20% of our premiums are ever actually paid back in claims. Ignore.

- **Extended Warranties**
The same advice applies to this form of insurance. The five year extension offered so persuasively by the major stores on your new TV, washing machine, computer etc, is never good value and rarely needed. They can add 50% to the cost of your purchase, and should be ignored at all times.

4. TELEPHONES

- **Land line**
We all have to pay BT rent for the land line, but, unfortunately, they are beaten on price by many competitors for use of that line, and so it pays to use one of their competitors for your calls. The best one for you depends on where and how many calls you make, but go into *uSwitch.co.uk*, and they will show you a choice of suppliers.

   With Broadband now the way into the Web for 10 million homes, dozens of suppliers offer their services at various prices. Check with *broadbandchecker.co.uk* for the comparisons of price and quality, as some are double the price of others.

   Quite separately, it is worth investigating VoIP, Voice over Internet Protocol, and suppliers like Skype. Making and taking your calls through the internet is growing fast, and the software needed is simple. There is no cost when you ring another VoIP customer, and little cost for other calls. If this is new to you, check on *VoIP.org.co.uk*, where the whole system is explained. Get all your friends around the world to sign up, and you can enjoy all your calls, however long, for no cost.

- **Mobile**
The mobile telephone market is so complicated that even most people in their shops don't understand it, but a few

hours research once a year can save a few hundred pounds. The best way to do that is to decide on the kind of telephone you want, the minimum number of minutes you expect to use it each month, and then investigate the market.

When you are ready, do your deal at the end of each month, when prices always fall. You can do it by wondering up and down the local High Street one Saturday morning, but far quicker is on the web, where the deals are easier to understand. Look at the main dealers' web sites, and then check out the web suppliers like *dialaphone.co.uk*.

For three mobiles recently we finished up with twice the number of minutes for half the High St. annual charges, and saved nearly £500. Not bad for 80 minutes work.

5. BANK ACCOUNTS

Unless you're one of the few who have a long-time friendly bank manager who will always be helpful, consider moving to Online banking.

The old banks rarely offer any interest on your current account, and, when they do, it is less than 1%. The new banks offer several per cent interest; some 40 times more than the High Street.

It's the same story on borrowing money. Old banks usually charge at least three times bank rate for overdrafts, and, when you go over, even for a day, this can often rise nearer 30%. If you go overdrawn by mistake by even a pound, they slap a £30–80 fine on you. UK banks make £3billion a year on unauthorised overdrafts.

Nor are they good value for any loans you may need. Far better value can be found on the list of personal loans available on the web; the superb *fool.co.uk* or the useful *thisismoney.co.uk* have the best list.

Whether you're lending the old banks money or borrowing from them, the costs are stacked against you, and hundreds of pounds a year can be easily saved by switching. Our generation often has the idea that there is still some mutual loyalty left in banks. Sadly, no. As elsewhere, new customers usually get treated much better than the old loyal ones.

6. CREDIT CARDS

When the banks started credit cards, they ceased to be professionals that we could trust; they became usurers. They borrow money for less than 4%, and then lend it to us for anything from 10 to 30%. Nice work, if you can get it.

It's now a huge business, and we owe over £56 billion on our 75 million cards. But there's no reason for you to join them. In fact, you can use credit card money to make a profit.

Here are some guidelines:

- Become a Card Tart and take advantage of the 0% transfer offers. Any money you don't need at the time can be invested so that, when you have to pay off that card, you will already have made a profit on it. Use these offers never to pay any interest on your credit card debts

- For your every day card, find one with the cheapest interest rate, so that, if you don't pay one month, the interest is small

- Never touch any store cards, the majority of which charge 20–30%

- Don't waste money withdrawing cash on credit cards

- Use low interest lifetime balance transfers when you need to run on any debts

- Pay off all card bills as early as possible

Most of us have to use credit cards these days, and the thing to do is to look on a money website – like the wonderful *moneysavingexpert.com* – and check the best deals for whatever purpose you need a card.

7. CREDIT RATING

At some time, many of us need to borrow money during the Third Act, and your credit rating is therefore important. All lenders have their own system for judging your worthiness, and they judge you according to the number of points you have. You get the most points if they can tick you against these:

- Over 45
- House owner
- Married
- Good record at bank
- Have telephone
- No County Court judgements
- No late payments on loan schedules
- No excessive applications for new credit cards – two a year is fine
- No bad news in your credit file as held by Experian. Check that by ordering a copy of your file for £2 (0115 976 8747)

8. CLASSIC CONSUMER TIPS

In earlier decades some of us were cavalier in our attitude to family budgets, but sensible purchasing of all goods and services can make a significant contribution.

- **Always shop around**. Check the competition's offer before you sign up for anything.

- **Use the Web**. It enables you to do your own market research and find the best deals without leaving your home.

- **Become a new customer**. Loyalty doesn't pay. New customers always get offered the best deals.

- **Monitor rates**. Suppliers change rates without your knowing, and never to your benefit. Monitor the interest rates on everything you're paying, like a mortgage, or receiving, as from savings funds.

- **Profit from special deals**. Everyone, from building societies to department stores, makes special offers part of their marketing. The 0% credit cards are typical of these.

- **Finally, don't get conned**. All that money you've so diligently saved can be lost to the temptations that flood in every day. Avoid them all.

  – Never join a Pyramid Scheme, *Give me £3000 today and you will get £12,000 in six weeks*. This is called a pyramid scam, and the first in may get their incredible profit, because they are getting the money that you and your friends put in later. There soon aren't enough people in the world to pay even your money back.

  – Never listen to a salesman from a Boiler room, who has been given your name as a serious investor and knows a wonderful share *that is about to double*. He's only trying to ramp it up, because he has a big stake.

  – Never take part in any scheme that *guarantees* more than 6% a year and your capital untouched; it has to be a scam.

  – Never send cheques *for admin purposes* to a phoney Lottery, because you have won a sweepstake in Toronto/Amsterdam/Dallas. They take your money and disappear.

  – Never reply to Nigerians bearing gifts, not even princesses. *As a Princess I want you to share £20 million*. No, she doesn't. She wants the details of your bank account, only to transfer your share of the money to you, she claims. But she will empty your account first. This is just one variation of the infamous Nigerian Scam, and some people have made the Princess very rich.

  You, of course, would never fall for any get rich quick scheme, but the sad truth is that most of us are conned at least once, and the crooks are reckoned to skim off some £370 million a year from the UK alone.

The reason why I suggest you spend a few hours a year managing your running costs is that it is well worth the time. In those few hours you might save thousands and will certainly save hundreds. Allocating a few hours every month can change your expenditure dramatically, and it is probably the easiest way of earning some fun money to pay for a few indulgences in your Grand Plan.

QUESTIONS

1. How much do you think you could save over a year if you did this audit?

2. Would you be happy to change your Bank account, your mortgage lender or your service suppliers?

3. Have you been approached by many Princesses?

CHAPTER 17

"Property is always a good investment, especially when tenants pay all your costs."

John Galsworthy

Could You be a Landlord?

A B2L scheme could be your alternative pension plan

So you've done the budgets for your Third Act; you've drafted your Grand Plan, you know the dreams that you want to fulfil. You've created a new balance of work and play. All is well in paradise. Except, maybe, for a slight concern over money 10 years or more down the road. It's the same old story; as costs grow and income falls, there's a need for new capital.

You are not alone. The vast majority of us didn't save enough to see us through a long Third Act, and any personal pension plans that you have are unlikely to produce the income you expected. It was disillusionment with these traditional pension schemes that forced many over the last decade to look for an alternative long-term investment.

And they found an answer. They became landlords, and started the Buy to Let (B2L) market back in the mid-nineties. They invested in a second property, where the rent aims to cover the annual costs, and the increased value, when you sell, is almost all yours to keep.

With the scrapping of regulated tenancies, risks to landlords were reduced, and mortgage lenders launched lower cost mortgages for the new breed of landlord. It was the perfect investment in a rising property market. The rapid growth in house prices enabled many investors to build up a large portfolio of flats and houses, as still more lenders came into the market, and mortgages became even cheaper.

This became known as the B2L game, and it's the hottest game in town. From nothing in '96, B2L has grown into a massive industry worth over £100 billion, and major developers often reckon that a third of their new flats are now bought by investors. Some 550,000 investors have already joined, and more thousands join each year. The majority have made good profits, and have seen returns of over 20%, from both income and capital growth.

For many people, becoming a property investor forms part of their Grand Plan. They want to keep working, but not for anyone else. They want to build up a business, but not one that leaves them no time for their dreams.

A part-time landlord could be the answer. Buy a B2L property, learn how to run it successfully, and, if you find it enjoyable work, build your property empire with a portfolio of rental homes.

And there's plenty of help. A flourishing market with over 30 Lenders offers a variety of mortgages, and the amount of money lent to the B2L investors is now around £20 billion a year, and rising.

There are two powerful reasons why so many have gone into the B2L market.

- First, it is heavily geared, and you may not need much capital to start. To buy a £200,000 B2L flat, you will probably be able to get a 75% mortgage, and so need only to put up £50,000. If you can re-mortgage your first home for that amount, then you could need only £10,000 for furnishings and buying costs.

- Second, when you sell, all the profits are yours to use in any way that is right for you. No forced annuities; none of your money kept by the insurance company. If your £200,000 B2L property doubles in value to £400,000, you net all the profit, less your mortgage loans, all perhaps for a £10,000 investment.

Sounds too good to be true? It does, but it has worked out that way for hundreds of thousands in the past. Is it a gamble? Of course it is. You are gambling on two factors:

- First, that the housing market will continue to rise, over a decade, as it has done during most of your lifetime.

- Second that the rental demand will continue to grow.

Are both these likely? History says Yes. Over the last 50 years property prices have doubled on average every ten years, with an average growth per year at 7–8%. This is almost as good as the stock market, but a far better return if you took advantage of the leveraging.

Secondly, the demand for rented property has been growing at some 10% a year, and there are valid social reasons for believing this will grow even faster.

But, of course, the market also goes through periods when prices fall. Those who invested in property at the end of the Nineties had an incredible rise for years. Some B2L investors saw their properties double in value in seven years from 1997 to 2004. Yet those who invested more recently have yet to enjoy much growth.

The whole B2L game is based on growth, and that is why the timing is particularly relevant to this investment, because it is unlikely to pay out any annual dividends. With a bit of luck, the rent will cover the costs of your mortgage, your expenses, the maintenance, the letting agency fees and those weeks when no one is renting. But don't expect any income over the years.

You aim to cover your costs, but paradise lies in the capital growth. However strong the demand for good rental properties, few investors expect to make any annual profit from their B2L properties.

Before you make your decision, I suggest that the first people you contact are ARLA, the Association of Residential Letting Agents, who specialise in advice on handling B2L properties. Their information is wonderfully comprehensive, and their excellent, free Buy to Let guide is obtainable from *arla.co.uk*.

I am a great fan of this organisation, simply because it is a source of sound facts and good advice at every stage, from what to buy and how to raise the money, to how to manage the business.

If you decide to go ahead, your first decision is obviously what to buy. Here are some basic principles.

12 Steps to Being a Successful B2L Investor

1. **Buy near to where you live**. A letting involves maintenance and personal attention at some time in the year, and the nearer you are the better.

2. **Buy what's easy to let**. This is a business proposition, not a personal choice. Never think *Would I live here?* Ask *Why would tenants live here?*

3. **Buy where the facilities are**. Buy in a mixed economy sector with lots of chimney pots. Always be near at least some shops, and transport. If you want a family let, check on the hospitals and schools; if you're looking for sharers, check on the restaurants and entertainment.

4. **Buy where the renters are**. Most renters are students, recent graduates in their first jobs, working singles, and the majority are under 35. Most are sharers. So buy in towns, and think first of terraced houses or flats.

5. **Buy a property with two bedrooms**. One or three bedrooms can rent well in some areas, but two bedrooms usually rent the fastest. Whether you need two bathrooms depends on the market you're aiming at, but a second bathroom can add considerably to the rent.

6. **Furnish the property to a high standard**. If you want to attract high quality tenants, pay particular attention to the attraction of the kitchen and bathroom.

7. **Remember that flats are easier to rent**. They give higher rental returns than houses, which will usually include gardens. As a rule, avoid anything, like a garden, that might require extra maintenance.

8. **Find a good local letting agent**. This is the most important ongoing member of your new team, who will know the rental potential, and will find your tenants. It is their responsibility to ensure the correct documentation is used, and, if you wish, they will also manage the property for you.

    The local market rent is key to your project, and your agent can tell you the realistic amount. Remember that only 10% of all tenants in the UK pay more than £250 a week; the average is £110. The average rental return is rarely more than 5% a year.

9. **Find a good mortgage broker**. They can guide you through the alternative mortgage options. Because the Lenders offer so many variations of mortgages, over three quarters of B2L investors get their mortgage through a broker, who can find the kind of loan that you need. Some specialise in first time investors; others are better for those building a portfolio of several properties.

10. **Find a good lawyer who knows the property business**. In case you have tenancy problems that need to be dealt with quickly, you need a lawyer who can act swiftly.

11. **Find a good accountant**. You will need him to advise you on the best structure for the project, as well as on the details of expenditure and revenue that he will need from you to ensure that you pay no tax.

12. **Prepare a Cash Flow statement**. When you have all your costs, do your budgets very seriously. Remember that two out of five lets last less than a year, and on average you should expect one void month a year with no rent coming in. You also need a reserve for sudden maintenance costs that can hit you at any time.

Realistic budgets are necessary, not just for you, but for your potential Lender. According to ARLA's statistics, over half its members buy with an interest-only mortgage, because they want the gearing to work for them. But, before agreeing to help you, every Lender wants to see your business plan, and, if they don't like it, they don't lend.

Most Lenders will grant you 75%, and some now will go to 85%, but they all want to see your budgets. What they require to check is that the genuinely obtainable rent covers at least 130% of the mortgage cost. That way the rent should be enough to cover both the mortgage repayments and the other inevitable costs of owning the property.

In other words, if your outgoing costs are £3000 a year, and your mortgage you want is going to cost £10,000 a year, then your obtainable rent must exceed £13,000 a year, or £280 a week for the 47 weeks rented. If your rent won't produce £13,000, then the Lenders will reduce the amount they are prepared to lend.

Can Anything Go Wrong?

It sounds simple. You study the rental market and invest in a sensible property in a good location. You find an efficient agent to keep it full of paying tenants, and manage it for you. Your broker finds you the right mortgage, and you cover your costs each year.

You have no income from it, but, on the other hand, it's not costing you anything. You are a player in the property game, looking forward to a killing several years down the line, when you sell.

So can anything go wrong? Of course it can. This is a business venture. The odds are historically in your favour, but, theoretically, it can go wrong for any of these reasons, The usual fears are these:

1. **The housing market collapses and dies**

   Possible in any short term, but unlikely over a decade. We are obsessed in the UK with buying our homes, and too few are built to satisfy this demand. Until they are built in their hundreds of thousands each year, there is no reason why prices should not continue, over the span of a decade, to rise by an average of 7% a year.

   A collapse can happen at any time, but B2L has to be seen as a long-term investment, and only 10% of B2L investors sell in less than five years. Historically, 30% of investors keep for 5–10 years; 40% keep the property for 10–20 years, and another 20% hold it for over 20 years.

   Of course, you may find that you bought at the wrong time and have to wait longer than you hoped for the price increase you expected. Equally, like those investors who bought in the second half of the Nineties, you might double your money in a few years.

   If you find that you have bought at the right time, and that this is an investment project that suits your needs, then you will soon realise that gearing, gearing, and gearing is the secret. With each increase in value, you can borrow further, against the extra collateral, to buy another property; and the result now is that over half of those investing in B2L have three or more properties.

   For the most part, little new investment is needed, as each new property can be bought on the back of the previous one's rise in value. With a portfolio of just three properties, you have the opportunity to sell one each five years, to keep your Grand Plan going without financial worries.

2. **The rental market collapses and dies**

   Why should it? Certainly, if we had an economic slump, then rents would fall, but the demographics are on your side.

- First time buyers of homes are now in their thirties giving you an extra decade of renters, who need those years to get on the property ladder.

- A third of the population lives alone, and it is forecast that it will be over four out of ten within the decade. Many of these will not want the problems of owning a home.

- Social housing is in decline. Traditional apartment blocks for key workers, like nurses and policemen, are being sold off by local councils for luxury development. This only adds to the demand for normal rentals.

- The student population is rising rapidly and studying longer.

- A growing divorce rate supplies more demand for renting at all ages, including millions in their Third Act.

- Job mobility is increasing, with new workers needing rented accommodation before they buy, and contract workers needing temporary homes for a fixed period.

- Immigration is increasing fast, and hundreds of thousands need to rent to start their English life.

Tenant demand is expected to grow 40% by 2010, but, even if your rentals aren't quite as much as you need in some years, and the property needs extra investment from time to time, this is no more than those failed pension policies that needed feeding every year.

3. **Interest rates leap higher**
   That would be seriously bad news, but all European govern-ments are geared to low inflation, and UK mortgage rates are already twice those of Europe or America. Even so, B2L investors need to ensure they can keep the project going, even if rates only go up slightly.

4. **You make a mess of it**

   Of course, you may make mistakes the first time around, but your team will help make it all happen. Investing in property is a business, and you, of course, are the one who has to make all the decisions. You have to do the initial work, decide the right area, find the right property, decide how it is furnished and painted.

   But, even if you initially make some wrong decisions, your team will be there to help. Your Lenders won't lend you the money to start, if they think your budget is wrong. Your estate agent will make sure that your revenue expectations make sense, and then can handle the ongoing management. Your accountant can check if your cash flow figures make sense.

5. **The taxman takes the profit**

   He takes some, but not much. The government will expect you to pay CGT, but the amount reduces the longer you own the property. After the third year the amount drops by 2% a year. So after 10 years a high rate taxpayer pays CGT at 24%.

   Against the profits you can set all your costs from Day One, all your improvement costs, and any losses you may have from any other investments, such as shares. You can, of course, then set your personal CGT annual allowances against your property profits.

   That's not all. If you move into the property for the six months before you sell, and declare it as your principal residence, that would qualify you for three years CGT-free. In addition you qualify for lettings relief of £40,000, and, after the taper relief, your CGT will be around 8%. Your accountant will come into his own here, but 8% rather than 40% is worth his fee.

At the very least, starting a new business as a landlord is worth investigating. Whatever you decide, the B2L game combines an interesting business proposition with a good long-term investment potential. Whether it fits into your Grand Plan, only you can decide, but it may be exactly what you need to bring fresh money into your plan at several stages. All you have to do is to buy the right property at the right time in the right place, and gather the right team to help you.

QUESTIONS

1. Would you enjoy being a landlord?

2. Do you believe that property values will double in 10 years?

3. Would you aim to gear up to a portfolio of properties?

4. Would you prefer to grow roses?

CHAPTER 18

"I keep a thermos flask of champagne. It's one of my little treats."

HM The Queen Mother

Are You a SKIer?

The Admen want to know if you are going to be a Big Spender (but aren't certain how to get at your money)

Well, are you going to be a SKIer? Are you going to be one of those members of the Third Act, who have decided that you only live once and you're going to use all the money you have to fulfil your dreams and enjoy every moment?

In other words, do you feel it your duty to leave as large an inheritance as possible to your children, or will you *Spend the Kids' Inheritance?*

The truth is, as you and I know, that we are rewriting the rules about the Third Act, as much as we did in the First Act. We invented 'Teenagers' as a marketable breed; now we've reinvented ourselves as the new Silver Wolves in our Third Act.

We just refuse to grow old. We decline the pipe and slippers, for the laptop and the flight over Everest. We start new companies, rather than visiting historic houses. We have no shame in wanting to look younger, acting young and enjoying life. We simply will not conform to some adman's notion that the world changes after 50.

We are not, in one sense, our parents' children. We do not go quietly into that dark night called 'Old', which has a pattern of life quite different from the years that came before. We do not adopt their attitudes; we adapt ours to a different age.

Does this mean that you might also become a SKIer? The

people who want to know are the marketing mafia. All those high-powered advertising men from Soho in London want to know if we're really going to spend some of the incredible wealth that, between us, we own.

You see, they have this dichotomy view about us, and it is worrying them. They know, because their research people have told them, that we are rich. Not individually, you understand, but as a generation. To start with, we apparently own some 80% of the nation's wealth, we are far richer than any other previous generation moving through the Third Act, and we already make up some 40% of the consumer spending.

We have between us some £270 billion of spending money. That they already know. The unknown is what we might spend on top of that in the future. It seems that we, in the Third Act of our lives, own property worth some £950,000,000,000 and rising – that's nearly one trillion pounds. That is dead money as far as they are concerned, because it is not real spending money, just house valuations.

But suppose that we could make some of that dead money real disposable money, then they very much want to be our friends. Which, of course, is what many of us are now doing. Through equity release schemes and lifetime mortgages (*see Chapter 15*), we are now bringing an extra billion pounds a year of disposable money onto the consumer market.

Not yet enough billions to excite some brand marketing managers, but Datamonitor, the research group which knows about these things, suggests that some £50 billion more pounds could well be released in this decade.

There's only one thing that could stop that money pouring into the market place. The kids. For thousands of years the parent/child relationship was constant. Parents looked after their children for the first 20 years; then the children looked after the parents for their last 20 years. That was the deal.

Then, over the last century, the attitudes changed. Parents became obsessed with leaving as much as they could to their children, even if it meant they lived in penurious circumstances to make it possible.

For many, now, the child/parent relationship has changed again. We're not asking our children to look after us, they say, but nor are we going to scrimp and save, so that they inherit a fortune, after we've lived in genteel poverty. We're going to borrow and spend, and they can have whatever's left.

They have looked at their children's lives, see that they are doing well, and have, therefore, decided that the children will not need a huge inheritance. They have decided to become SKIers, Spenders of the Kids' Inheritance.

If you are tempted to join them, but feel any guilt about this decision, this can usually be assuaged by any of the following arguments:

- The kids don't actually need it, they're doing so well. More than that, for heavens sake, they are richer than we ever were.

- We on the other hand do need it. We've worked hard for 30/40 years, we've sacrificed our lives to give them a good start in life, and now we deserve a bit of fun.

- With the Government taking 40% inheritance tax on anything over, say, £300,000, it's really not worth leaving much more money behind for them.

- The house will double in value by the time we go, so they'll get their inheritance from the house. I mean, if house prices go on like they have through our middle years, then they'll be fine, whatever we spend.

But, how will you, if you become a SKIer, spend your money? That's the other question the great manufacturers and their advertising agencies want to know. Are you going to be in the market for their goods? Can they persuade you to change your washing powder, your car, your clothes?

Only, I suspect, if they change their perception of us right now. I offer two lists that support that point.

According to the survey by YouGov, the top ten Wishes of what they called the Nifty Fifties (*see Chapter 20 for the names people call us; it's very confusing*) are these:

- **Travel round the world**
- **Swap the safe family car for a high-powered convertible and drive through Italy**
- **Have a steamy affair**
- **Take part in ocean yacht racing**
- **Fly a plane or, at least, take up sky diving**
- **Go white water rafting**
- **Attend concerts of the famous pop groups of earlier days**
- **Own a champion stallion**
- **Write a best-seller, based on one's personal experience**
- **Become a monk for a month**

There seems to be to be a touch of the male menopause in the list, but, as Sherlock Holmes famously said, the key point is that the dog did not bark. The key point here is that there is nothing in this Wish List about chair lifts in a home near a hospital.

Whatever you may feel about that list, it is not one that could have been made up by an Ad agency. I recently saw a list in an agency, where the copywriters had been asked to put down the products that, they thought, could best be promoted to the 55Plus market. The list read as follows:

- **Stair lifts** (*see what I mean?*)
- **Easy-to-wear clothes and shoes**
- **Medical drugs**
- **Nostalgic 'Best Of' compilation CDs**
- **Horlicks type drinks**
- **Korean cars**
- **Charities**
- **Beauty creams**
- **M & S**
- **Garden centres**

Could any list be so wrong? I personally enjoy two of these ten, but it does illustrate fairly dramatically how far from reality is the marketing man's perception of us.

Mind you, the Press are just as confused. They sometimes write about us as if all 20 million of us were rich. Here come the 'Silver Surfers' shouts one headline, describing how we're the 'new young', with money to spend on anything.

Then, often only a few pages later on, the paper bemoans the fate of the 'poverty pensioners', suggesting that we're all living lonely lives in bedsits, and the only time we ever go out is to the hospital.

This latter attitude is unfortunately not helped by the names of two most important historical organisations, *Help the Aged* and *Age Concern*. They are both distinguished bodies, and both make an enormous contribution with their lobbying and information, but their names do reflect the 'poor pensioner' attitude.

The truth is that we are, as a generation, as financially mixed as we ever were. For almost half of us in the Third Act, money is not plentiful, nor ever has been. For maybe a couple of million there are no money problems, except how to spend it. The rest of us are not rich, but we have some money to spend, and this is what the marketing mafia are hoping to grab.

Until recently, they remained convinced that the young were the only people in the world with money. Few advertising campaigns were aimed at us; even fewer manufacturers ever come out and said that their product was just about right for those of us in the Third Act of life.

Now, they're wondering if they had better think again. They keep on reminding themselves of three factors. First, we are going to get even richer as we broker our homes for disposable cash. Second, every year another quarter of a million enter their Third Act, and so the market keeps growing. Thirdly, we will be the beneficiaries of inheritances from our parents, as we get older.

But, if they do want our money, they will have to learn a bit more about us and the way we are. Most people in advertising are at least one generation younger – often two – and hold stereotype images of 'older' people that belong more to the age of our fathers.

As the marketing men increasingly decide that they do want a share of your spending money, and encourage you to become a SKIer, I suggest they might do worse than remember a few things about us:

Eleven Characteristics of the Third Act Consumers

1. **We do not really change products easily**. They will have to find good reasons to make us change, not just meaningless cartoons and loud music. If we liked something when we were 40, we probably like it at 60, whether it be a brand of jeans or electric shaver, but we can be wooed to change, if they speak to us in a more civilised way.

2. **We are in the market for quality**. We want things that reflect the quality of life that we now think we deserve. We are downsizing our lives and want quality, not quantity. We want things with a long shelf life, not passing fancies.

3. **We are nostalgic** in some ways, and do enjoy compilations of great hits by our favourite entertainers and film stars (one of the few things the agency copywriter got right).

4. **We use the mute button**. We may watch a bit more TV than before, although of course we always deny that, but usually press the mute button when the TV ads come on. We are more likely to get our information from newspapers and radio, and notice advertising more while reading than viewing.

5. **We are healthier than our parents' generation** and have little interest in most health drugs advertising. What we are interested in are fitness techniques, diets, and lifestyles that will help to keep us young and fit. We have no intention of going easily into old age.

6. **We love the Web**. We have taken to technology almost seamlessly and buy more on the net than our children do. We already spend an average of £500 a head on line each year.

7. **We want simple toys**. We use the computer, the mobile phone, and endless silver boxes in both work and play. But we want simple efficiency and convenience, not complicated technology with endless add-ons that we're never likely to use, and which will often go wrong.

8. **We like eating out, but we also cook**. We may be the last generation in the country that actually cooks. We love the microwave, self-starter ovens, good cutlery, American fridge/freezers, and anything that makes entertaining easier.

9. **We love to travel**. We want to see more of the world than we ever did before, but there must be an element of adventure and exploration, and we don't want to bunk down in walk-ups. We enjoy a touch of luxury.

10. **We love property**. We are always interested in a home in the sun, exchange homes, new décor ideas; we love most property and all the fun that goes with it. After all, it's what made most of us most of our money.

11. **We don't like to be patronised**. We will certainly not respond to any patronising message, or any suggestion that the problem, for which their product is a cure, comes only to older people. People in their Third Act do not see themselves as a species apart.

Most of us, I suspect, will not become extreme SKIers and spend *all* our children's inheritance. You may no longer think of it as a sacred duty, but you will hope to leave them something.

Equally you are not going to deny yourself the achievement of your dreams, or the fulfilment of your Grand Plans. You will spend money, and, if it runs out, you will be tempted to raise more from your domestic equity.

The one thing that the marketing people can be certain about is that you are going to spend much more money than your parents. You may not spend it in quite the way they hoped, but that's something they will have to learn as you enjoy life your way.

QUESTIONS

1. Would you be happy becoming a SKIer?

2. If you did, what would you spend your money on?

3. What kind of advertising do you respond to?

Twelve Top Travel Experiences

More travel is a wish for most in their Third Act, and you might like to check your choices against this List of the 10 most wanted travel experiences. It comes from a survey of European men aged 55–65.

- Take a helicopter down the Grand Canyon
- Sledge down the Cresta
- Play golf at Augusta
- Fly in a hot-air balloon over an African safari park
- Spend a month on a tropical island
- Gamble at Las Vegas
- Scuba dive in the Great Barrier Reef
- See Venice from a gondola
- Take a world cruise
- Swim with the dolphins

CHAPTER 19

"The sun is the best rejuvenating power of all."
Somerset Maugham

Your Home in the Sun

Time to make one dream come true

O ne out of four people in their Third Act expect to have a home in the sun by the end of the decade, and the idea of a second home in a different world has become part of the dream in the Third Act. Get it right, and it is more than a dream; it has been a very good investment for hundreds of thousands. For these two good reasons I include a chapter on buying a home abroad in *Silver Wolf*.

If you have the same dream in your Grand Plan, the good news is that a home abroad is now more feasible than ever. There are more places to choose from, it is simple to keep in touch with the family and friends, and the money is comparatively easy to borrow.

Whatever you choose, you will not be alone. It is reckoned that over a million already have their place in the sun. A few live there full time; some only for winters; but the majority use the home just for holidays, while they continue to work in the UK – although thousands who do still work in the UK now commute from their places in Spain or France.

No one knows exactly how many live where, but the French say that about 360,000 Britains have homes in their country, although, of course, they can't resist the dig that these are mainly homes in the countryside, where the French have no desire to live.

The Spanish believe that 630,000 of us have a home there, from the Costa Brava south to the Costa del Sol. These, in contrast to France, are mainly in the coastal districts.

The Portuguese reckon there are 65,000 of us, mainly along the Algarve, and partly along the Estoril coast near Lisbon.

For all the talk of the Brits having turned Tuscany into Chiantishire, the Italians don't know of more than 30,000 of us as actual property owners in the whole country. Add a few thousands in Greece and Turkey, maybe 15,000 in Florida, and that estimate of 1.1 million seems about right.

If that seems unexpectedly high to you, you may be even more surprised by the forecast that another million will buy a home in the sun this decade, and then double that in the years after 2010.

At the moment, around 150,000 buy each year, but, by 2020, the forecast is that one in four of us in our Third Act will be living, at least for part of the year, in our second home abroad.

One of the reasons, according to recent *Alliance & Leicester* research, for this new exodus abroad will be that foreign governments will soon entice us, through tax breaks and easy mortgages, to come to their country.

We are going to be a targeted market, because foreign governments already see in us a great source of new income. '*British retirement migrants will be worth nearly £50 billion a year, and we need this money*' according to one Spanish minister. I'm not certain I like being called a '*retirement migrant*', but it will be pleasant to be given a generous welcome.

The traditional reason for the old exodus was, of course, the sun, which explains why nine out of ten people have bought into sunny regions. Living in the warmth is a kind of liberation from the cold, buttoned-up working life in most of Northern Europe.

But I think there's always been a much more powerful reason. Making a new home in another country also gives you the chance to have a different kind of life. In your home in the sun, you have no history, no pattern of life to which others expect you to conform. It provides a new stage for you to play out some of the scenes in your Grand Plan.

Some of those who actually live most of the year in their second home suddenly become part-time farmers, renovating old *fincas*, and hoeing arid land. They buy vineyards, and dream of the day when the grapes produce enough for the bottles to have their name on them.

They set up small businesses, from language schools to marina management, and they open *'gites'*. They run painting courses, and open cookery schools. They learn to speak a second language, they sail a yacht, build a house.

Of my own friends, I can think of one couple, who go to their Provençal ranch three times a year for six weeks at a time, and paint. He now has his watercolours in galleries, both in France and the UK. An ex-banker in the Algarve has become a golf addict and plays three days a week in winter, but also now plays piano three nights a week in his local hotel; his ex-barrister wife runs an interior design agency.

Two richer friends have become property developers in their own right. One in the Loire actually does have a vineyard with a small chateau of a dozen rooms, and produces some 5,000 bottles a year. Another, somewhat bizarrely, bought a house near Arles, which had its own bullring. He now puts on Provençal bullfights, in which no bulls are killed or even hurt.

How the Dream became More Possible

Owners of homes abroad have all taken their chance to live a life quite different from the one that filled their Second Act. They have taken advantage of the three key factors that make the home in the sun dream easier in every way – the value of their UK property, the rise of the Web, and the arrival of the low cost airlines.

Between them, these three have made possible the money to buy the second home, diminished any guilt at being away from the family for any long periods, and opened up lands that once took too long to reach.

1. The Web

The laptop and the internet have reduced the guilt you might have felt at being away from family and friends, by making it easy to stay in touch.

You can send messages that will arrive thousands of miles away within minutes. You can receive photos of the family with a simple attachment to the email. You can telephone on line with Skype for no cost. You can set up video conferencing that will make it seem that they are in the room.

Suddenly the computer has broken the geographical barriers, and made it possible to be *en famille*, wherever you are. As more people use the Web to its full potential, so will more of us realise what it makes possible.

The web also means that you can find and research your overseas home while you are still in your UK home. Type the words "houses to buy in Charentes", or "islands for sale in Croatia", and you will be given pages of properties for sale as agents show off what is on their books. You can refine your search, until you have some idea of the market without moving.

Finally, and on a practical working level, the web makes it possible for you to work from the sun, without being in the UK office every day. In the south of Spain, for example, they estimate that some 25,000 British people are already doing just that, using the cheap and frequent flights to get back to the UK, when needed in person. Most days they run their companies from their home abroad through sophisticated technology.

2. Your UK house value

The unique experience of a 10-year property boom has made many rich, even if their bank manager doesn't think so. Most homes have more than doubled in value in the last 10 years, and you can use the value of your UK home as extra collateral for a mortgage to pay for the home in the sun.

Or, you can use the new valuation to raise the capital through an equity release scheme (*see chapter 15*). If a home in the sun was a dream of yours, you can now make it happen, by leveraging your largest asset.

3. Low cost airlines

The arrival of the low-cost airlines, led by Easyjet and Ryanair, has had a dramatic effect on the price of air travel. They are the great heroes of the second home dream.

The old state airlines charged fortunes to fly us anywhere, but, once the low cost airlines arrived, with fares at under half the old price, they too were forced to lower their ticket prices, and so all air travel with any airline became cheaper.

Just as important was the low cost airlines' opening up of new routes. The old airlines flew only to the big cities; the new breed flies into smaller cities, and makes it easy for us to move into new regions.

So, computer literacy removes any guilt; new house values give you the power to raise the money; the low cost airlines make flying to Malaga or Carcassonne often cheaper than the train from London to Leeds or Liverpool. All you have to do now is decide what kind of home you want.

You really can buy whatever you want and can afford. Go through the papers and magazines and hundreds of web sites, and the choice is amazing. In the week when I wrote this, I found a chateau with 30 bedrooms and two bathrooms in Burgundy, a vineyard in Cyprus, and a stable complex for 60 horses outside Sevilla. I could buy a 'country' in Dubai's The World development, a *finca* in Mallorca, or half an island off the Croatia mainland.

If none of those appealed, there was a baroque apartment on the Isle S. Louis in Paris, a six-bedroom villa behind Marbella, or a hotel suite in the Emirates. An Art Deco apartment on the South Beach in Miami; a studio in Lucca with panoramic views but 55 steps; and half a Crusader's ruin in the Peleponnese were three more possibilities. Apart from these, you could choose from over 100,000 more normal apartments in sensible developments all along the Mediterranean coasts.

What kind of Home in the Sun do You want?

If this is a life-changing decision – and it certainly is if you intend to spend an increasing part of your time there at some time in the future– it's worth being absolutely clear as to what you want to buy to fulfil your dreams.

There's much to be decided, and it helps if you are clear on what exactly you want. Here are some questions that might lead to the right choice for you.

1. **Why do you want a home in the sun?**

   Is it an investment, a foreign B2L, or simply for your pleasure to spend longer holidays there each year? Is it for living in for much longer periods in future years? Do you want somewhere away from the world, or do you want to live in the heart of city life?

   Depending on your answers you may want a farmhouse in the hills, or a front line flat on the beach; a villa of your own, or a penthouse tucked into community; a renovated palazzo or an old townhouse. The choice of homes is enormous, but only you know which kind is your dream.

2. **What climate do you want?**

   Check the weather charts, especially for the periods you will initially want to spend there. It's not always hot, and the sky is not always blue. Tuscany is often too hot in high summer, but by the autumn it's raining and cold. The Greek islands can be idyllic for five months, then stormy from October onwards.

   Brittany and Normandy have worse winters than the UK; even Provence often has the Mistral and snow in winter. Much of central and northern Spain is freezing in winter; and, if you really want to throw away your winter over-coats, you have to go to Florida or Cape Town for guaranteed sunshine.

3. **Do you want your own villa in your own grounds, or to live in a development?**

   Private villas are often the first dream. You are king of your estate; you have your own pool, BBQ and garden, and, if you ever decided to rent it, you can ask double the rent of the same size house in a development.

Privacy is the great advantage, but it comes at a price. It's you who has to run the place, and that's now expensive (forget the myth about cheap labour). It also means that you are not living within any social community, and have no day to day relationship with others.

Do you want to be on your own, or would you prefer to have others around? If that's important to you, then you may prefer a development. This is likely to have more facilities than your private villa, and all the landscaping, the maintenance, satellite TV, and the pool are not your worry. But, of course, you share the pool with others, and you still have to pay your share of the community charge.

4. **Do you want the beach and the town, or the countryside and the village?**
    This is more a matter of lifestyle than money. To live in the countryside doesn't mean you need to be far from a beach or town when you want them.

    In most areas you will need a car to travel around, whichever you choose, but in town beachside developments you can often forget the car, because your amenities are all around you.

    This is what most people want, and so this is easiest to sell when you want a change. All surveys show that the majority of buyers want to see the sea and to have amenities at hand.

    On the other hand, you usually get a lot more for your money in the countryside, and it is much easier to become part of the local life. This is especially true in France, where 'mad' Brits are known for buying old houses in old villages, and Conranising them into elegant '*gites*'.

5. **How long are you prepared to travel?**
    Broadly, you have three choices. Somewhere needing a day to fly there; a place that takes half a day; or a second home near enough to drive to for a long weekend.

    • The reason why over two-thirds go to Mediterranean coasts is that the Rivieras and the Costas fit perfectly into what most want. They are warm and only half a day away. Catching the 7am flight gets you to your house for lunch; when you leave, get an evening flight back, and you're home before midnight. In emergency, there are dozens of flights a day to get back to the UK.

- The reason for the British invasion of Brittany and Normandy is that you can go by car, and often reach your second home in less time than it takes to reach Cornwall. The weather may be no better, but the food makes up for it. France is often the first choice of those who love to pack the car and avoid airports. With the Eurotunnel and the new motorways, the time has halved.

- For those wanting to use their second home for longer stays, or even the whole winter, a day's travelling is no drawback, and so opens up Florida and Cape Town as possibilities.

6. **Would you prefer a new or old region?**
   By which I mean the choice between an established area, or one that is still hoping to become popular. This doesn't necessarily mean going to a new country.

- In Spain, the Costa Blanca and Costa del Sol are packed with ex-pats, but the Costa del Luz, west of Gibraltar, and the Costa del Azahar, south of Valencia, are less crowded and often a third cheaper.

- In France, the Cote d'Azur has been in demand for 80 years and prices reflect this. At the western end of the French Mediterranean coast, people have only really discovered the Rousillion and Languedoc in the last 10 years, and prices are, again, a third less. The Dordogne was colonised by the English 20 years ago, but the Charente has hardly been touched and gives you far more for your money.

- In Italy, English families dot across many Tuscany hills, but Umbrian hill towns, like Gubbio, still have secret homes under

£100k. As usual, colonisation is following the airlines, and Le Marche is now ripe for development, with the flights into Pescara and Ancona. Gourmets are now buying in Bologna.

- In Florida, most of the early money went into Orlando and areas around Disney world, and then down to Miami, but it is the west coast of southern Florida that is getting the clever money, north and south of Naples.

- Croatia and Bulgaria are suddenly being tipped as future Rivieras, cheap now, but good enough to double in price, once the flights are plentiful and the infrastructure is completed in four years time. Both have had their hopes raised before, but this time Croatia has already got its sprinkling of stars, from Sir William Gates of Microsoft fame to Michael Douglas, both buying islands; and Dubrovnik is one of Europe's great cities.

- The biggest new player is Dubai, where the world is being redrawn in the Gulf, as palm leaves of islands offer everything from a studio at £100k to an 8000sq.ft. villa for a million and more.

7. **Do you want a new or resale home?**
   If it is an investment and you are in no hurry, then buying new, off-plan, has often been the first choice. The only concern is if the developer fails to finish the agreed development. This is why you will always want to employ a lawyer before you buy anything anywhere, not only to ensure your money is secure, but you are covered for any failings by the developer.

   Buying an existing home doesn't have that worry, but nor does it have any built-in rise in value. The great advantage of buying an existing home is the same as everywhere; you can inspect it, and see the facilities that are already with it.

8. **Do you want to rent it out?**
   If it's only for your pleasure, you can obviously buy whatever

you choose, but, if you also want some rent to help pay the mortgage and costs, when you are not there, you may want to consider what rents more easily:

- Renters like flight travel to be direct and under three hours from the UK

- Renters like the property to be under an hour from the airport. (Over an hour, and you lose 25% of the potential market; over 90 minutes you lose half)

- Renters like to have amenities within walking distance

- Developers often exaggerate the amount of rent you can expect, but, if you buy the right property, in the right area, with the right facilities, your rental returns in the summer months can make a considerable contribution towards paying for your basic costs

---

"Property is a game and you have to know how to play it"

Jack Cotton

Once you've decided clearly what you want for your dream, all you have to do is buy it. There is no great mystery to buying abroad, but I have to tell you, as part of a family which has had homes in Tuscany, Southern Florida, the Côte d'Azur and Andalucia, that it is very easy – and very expensive – to get it wrong.

Most people do get it right, and enjoy a second home that adds to their lives, opens up a new world, and has been a wonderful investment on top, but here are some tips that I have learnt over the years. Most of them are obvious, but some may be particularly relevant for your decision.

The Silver Wolf 12 Tips on Buying Your Home in the Sun

1. **Work with a local agent and know your prices**

   No other market is quite like that of the UK, where prices are well-known to most people. In second home markets in the sun, only a good local estate agent knows exactly what the real market price is, and what's available.

   The first thing to find out from the agent is the cost per square metre. For example, if you're looking for a basic two bed, two bath apartment within 100 sqm, and the going rate in your chosen area is £1000 psm, then you know that you will probably have to pay around £100,000.

   That price is then increased or decreased according to its situation and advantages. As you will soon find out in your own research, prices can vary enormously within a short distance. A flat in an old development can be going for 200,000 euros, while, 400 metres across the valley, the new estate doesn't have anything under 300,000.

   Asking prices can vary dramatically, depending on how badly the owner, both private and developer, wants to sell.

   Beware of unscrupulous operators posing as legitimate salespeople or agents. Never go alone to remote areas or villas to view. Check the contacts you deal with.

2. **Get a bilingual lawyer**

   An extraordinary fact is that the first wave of second home buyers hardly ever used a lawyer, and a great number ended up in a mess. Contrary to the impression given by TV prog- rammes, it is not simple to buy in any country, and few of us can do it without a good lawyer. Spain is difficult enough, but France is even worse.

   Your lawyer will stop you signing things like the *compromis de vente*, which commits you to completing within 60 days; insist on the right wording in *conditions suspensives*; deal with the *notaire* and know what to do when the *notaire* leaves the room.

In any country you need the lawyer to be certain that the vendor actually owns the property. Many are the horror stories in Umbria of the 19th son from Sicily arriving to claim his inheritance, a day after you move in.

Many are the tales in Spanish villages of foreigners buying cottages sold with debts; debts in Spain being usually not on the vendor, but on the house. Many recently are the horror stories from Croatia of deeds held by some authority and not released.

You need your lawyer also to make certain that you are covered if any problem arises. He will stop you signing any piece of paper until he is certain that the deal is kosher; too many people have been caught by developers' failure to complete, or by local government officials' incompetence.

Most importantly of all, you need your lawyer to advise you on the best way to formalise ownership of the property, offshore or on shore, company or private, one owner or many. There are tax implications to each decision.

3. **Find a mortgage broker to help the financing**
   Mortgages are not difficult to get in most countries, but the rules are different, and you need a helping hand.

- Most banks are happy to lend two thirds of the value, and some up to 75%, but don't expect more.

- The amount you can borrow is usually not a multiple of your income, but worked out so that the repayment costs are no more than a third of your net income.

- You can borrow against the value of the second home, or re-mortgage your main home and use that as collateral.

- Whichever way you raise a mortgage, expect to need at least 45% of the value in cash. This is for payment of the part not covered by the mortgage, say 30%, plus 10% buying costs, plus 5% furnishings.

- The big decision is which currency. Even if you raise the mortgage against your UK house, some Lenders will grant euro or dollar mortgages, but the risk, of course, is whether the currency you choose moves against you down the years.

  Right now the temptation is to take foreign currencies, where the mortgage rate can be nearly half the UK rates. However, unless you're hoping to use rental income to pay the mortgage, you have the danger of having to exchange pounds at a rate that could easily change by 10% the wrong way.

4. **Get it right first time**

   Buying and selling in Europe or America is far more expensive than in the UK. Buying costs in Spain and Florida are just over 10%; in France nearer 20%. Agent's costs and CGT make it even worse when you sell.

   Getting it wrong, and having to sell and then buy again, is not only wasted time, but a very expensive start. You have notary fees, transfer taxes, agent's fees, lawyer's fees, mortgage arrangement costs, and an endless list of tiny payments.

   The worst mistakes have been made by those on a weekend inspection trip, who fell in love with a house on the Saturday, put down a deposit on the Sunday, and realise by Wednesday that it wasn't what they wanted.

   Once you've decided on the country and the region, my recommendation is that you stay in different areas for a week at least. Even if you decide on one coast, like Andalucia, there are dozens of different worlds in a province that is nearly as large as the UK.

5. **When you've found your home, bargain**

   From Miami to Marbella it's a negotiating game. Bidding is a serious part of that game, and I have known many properties go for a third off the asking price, simply to get them sold. It's often done with charm and wine, and there's always a time for negotiating on furniture, legal costs, kitchens, etc.

   Then, remember that it is *always* a buyers' market. At any one time there are thousands of properties for sale, and some owners are always desperate to sell. The property salesman may claim to have the greatest bargain of all time, but there's usually another one down the road.

This applies particularly to resales. There are enormous bargains in the resale market, simply because there is a lot of competition, some people need to sell quickly, and the owners are often back in England.

Once you've homed into your area of interest, you may well find your resale dream from asking in cafés and bars. Or drop into the ubiquitous English or Irish Pub, where ex-pats are often to be found. They usually have a good network, and know what's for sale, and, more pertinently, who needs to sell.

6. **Buy a premium site**
   In two words that means Front Line. Buy the front line over-looking the sea; buy the front line onto the golf course. Buy where there are good facilities, where the infrastructure works. These are always dearer than other properties, but they increase their value faster, and they can, one day, if necessary, be sold more easily.

7. **Buy off plan**
   With new developments, if you buy off plan, you will, usually, get a lower price than buying your home when it is completed. The developer needs cash flow; you get a discount. This works particularly well, if it will be built in several stages. Buying early, you not only get the best site, but, by the time the development is finished, and you actually move in, your home should be worth more.

   There is, of course, always a risk investing in a home that does not exist, and you need your lawyer to ensure you are covered by a bank guarantee.

   You can, paradoxically, often get a very good deal if you are among the last to buy. If there is still a home already built that you would like, then make an offer; the developer is usually very keen to end the project. This is particularly true of the show flat, much seen but never slept in. If you like it, bid low, in return for letting them continue to show it until you arrive.

8. **Buy on the sea side of any coast road**
   Where a road runs along the coast – such as in the Costa del Sol, or most of the south of France – property on the beach side is always the best buy. Property on the "wrong" side of the road, on the country side, usually costs less than the sea side, but it is more difficult to sell.

9. **Buy a view of the sea**
   Most future buyers and renters will want to see the sea. You may wonder why, and it may not be important to you, but take it as a fact. Even if it is miles away up in the hills, it must have a view of the sea. They also want to have cafés and shops near them, be within an hour of the local airport, and within 10 minutes of a beach or pool.

10. **Follow the low-cost airlines**
    Anyone looking to make an early profit on their home abroad should find out where the airlines are opening up new routes, because that's where prices rise fast.

    The most dramatic example is probably south west France, where homes were half the price of those on the other side of Marseille. After Ryanair started flying to Montpellier, Carcassonne, and other towns in the region, property prices have risen by over 20% a year.

    All over Europe new low-cost airlines are now spreading cross the continent, and opening up new territories. As the new airlines open routes to Croatia, we'll pour in. The same could apply to Bulgaria, Romania and most of the Eastern Europe countries, as well as Greece and Turkey.

11. **Don't expect life to be very much cheaper**
    These days it is often a myth that life is cheaper abroad. In 2006, if you really want cheaper living, then Spain is still 15% below ours, and Miami 10%, but Tuscany is almost identical. France is 18% dearer, and Australia, our most favourite country outside Europe, is 20% dearer. If the cost of living seriously affects your decision, South Africa currently offers the best deal at 40% less than UK costs.

Currency fluctuations may also affect where you buy. In 2004–5 Florida became cheap, as the dollar got nearer to two to the pound, and thousands took advantage of the chance to benefit from that. This has now changed, but those who did buy then have a double bonus of currency appreciation and property price boom. The rand rate is still encouraging buyers in Cape Town, but the strengthened euro made European homes 10% dearer over 2005–6.

Health facilities once affected the living costs, but today Spain and France are better than the NHS in many regions, and we now have full reciprocal services throughout Europe, However, Florida's medical services can be crippling, unless you have a full insurance policy, which could cost £10,000 for a couple.

12. **Don't expect ridiculous prices**

Finally, don't expect property prices to be half those in the UK. Prices have boomed everywhere in the last five years, and in 2002–5 Spanish prices, for example, rose more than British. Gone are the days when you could buy a home abroad for half the equivalent cost in the UK.

These days it's just as easy to pay a million euros for a home along the Mediterranean, as it is in the UK, but most of us don't. The majority of homes in the sun cost under 250,000 euros, and 500,000 can buy serious luxury, but it is now rare to find something ready for immediate use in a developed region under 150,000 euros.

This doesn't mean that there aren't thousands of cottages across Europe under this price, but very few are ready for you to move straight in. Yet the good news remains that you can get far more property for your money almost anywhere in Europe than in the UK.

Whatever home in the sun you eventually buy, and whether you live in it for half the year, or have full on-going lives in the UK and can only get away for short periods, it offers you a life style that is far removed from that back home. But it is more than that. Most homes in the sun have historically been a good investment, What other indulgence has claims to be so life-changing, so enjoyable, and also so profitable?

QUESTIONS

1. Do you have a dream to spend part of your year in the UK and part abroad?

2. How would you raise the money to buy a home in the sun?

3. Which country would you choose for its language, food, and life style?

4. Or, does just the thought of being with other nationalities for more than a fortnight horrify you?

CHAPTER 20

"Just remember, once you're over the hill, you pick up speed."

Charles M Schultz

Join the Club

You do not belong to any group; you are a Silver Wolf

In a world no longer defined by class but by socio-economic groups, governments, sociologists and marketing men love to give names to each group. They don't see the world as being full of individuals, but belonging to a collection of markets. So they try to pigeonhole you into one of their markets. Ignore them.

As far as you are concerned, the fifties is simply the time you become a player in your Third Act, the age when you begin the Grand Plan for your next 20 years. It is an important moment in your life, and the beginning of what should be the best years of our lives. But it doesn't put you into some new social group.

Nevertheless, for their different reasons, governments, sociologists and marketeers are determined to label us in their attempt to define who and what we are.

Most of their groups are age-related; some more attitude related. Some may annoy you; others are marginally acceptable. I include them here only as a reminder of their attempts to pigeonhole all of us.

* 50 Plus

This is the youngest age group. I am not certain who started it, but the insurance companies use it a lot to indicate that we are now infinitely more responsible, and so qualify for cheaper insurance.

Several web sites also aim at what they call the Fifty Plus or over50 group, and are worth googling for a lot of useful help.

This is also the age when many in the public sector start drawing their pension, much to the annoyance of those in the commercial world. Those with personal pension plans can withdraw their tax-free 25% from this age, and leave the rest of the policy to grow.

* Nifty Fifties

Other marketing men call you the Nifty Fifties. That name focuses on those who start their new Third Act life with a flurry, and spend their money on adventurous living, presumably in the belief that they wont be fit enough to do the same when they're older. The travel industry is particularly keen to get their money.

Market research people sometimes use the term **MOFS**, Male over Fifty Spenders. They claim that this group is having the time of its life, buying mainly tech toys, and can often be persuaded to fork out for a new silver car.

By the time you read this they'll probably have drawn up a new acronym for that.

* 55 Plus

This Group started in America, where they developed housing, particularly in sunny States like Florida and California, designed to fit the assumed lifestyles of the traditional retiree. The basic qualification for living in these estates was that you had to be at least 55 years old.

Many of them do not allow children to live there, nor do they allow owners to rent. At their best these villages are havens for those who want a quiet life and their own independence, supported by on-site care; at their worst they become single age group ghettos.

Where it often best works in America is where the estate is built around a country club and golf course, with as many sporting and social activities as any other development.

The age of 55 will also be the proposed minimum age for drawing any pension after 2010.

* 60 Plus

At this stage all women still join the ranks of pensioners, and no longer have to make any national insurance contributions. Pensioner is a once-noble name, given to those who had served their country well. Unfortunately, it is now too often used to indicate those whom society wishes to condemn to a life of non-working. It has come to have a derogatory connotation, a never-quite-said, but usually assumed, hint of second class citizenship.

Never let anyone call you a pensioner.

* Old Age Pensioner

This is the final Group that we all come under from the age of 65, when men also officially become pensioners. By this age all men and women receive a State Pension of varying amounts, all pathetic. Whether you add to this munificence by cashing in on your own pension funds is up to you.

This is also the age when most organisations will expect you finally to leave. Not because you are incompetent, but because you are 65. Not even the abolition of age discrimination will give you any right to stay on, but at least you can now apply for an extension.

Hopefully, in a few years you will not qualify to be called a pensioner until you are at least 70, but right now this is the age you officially join that club.

Just to confirm the significance of that word, someone in Whitehall thought of putting three words together, so that, from this age, you become an Old Age Pensioner. Which has to be on a par, as a put down, as calling someone a Spotty Faced Kid.

The PR department hastily turned it into an acronym, OAP. So beaten down was the previous generation that they accepted this condescending acronym, but we will have it thrown away into the overstocked pond of discarded Whitehall misnomers.

However, there is one financial advantage to being 65. The government awards all men in the OAP Group with a tax rise. They will no longer take any National Insurance contribution of 10% or 6% from you. You have now paid your dues.

* Silver Surfers

Sociologists in America created a smaller Group, known as the Silver Surfers, which followed the discovery that people over 60 bought more on the web than those younger.. Silver surfers are an important group to some advertisers, who realise that surfers have a lot of spending money, and they would like some of it.

Unfortunately, in the UK, only a quarter of those over 65 are computer literate, but this is more than made up by those in the 50–60 age group, where 45% are constant users of the Web. They are now the biggest spending surfers of any decade.

* SKIers

Every advertiser loves the **SKIers**, the people we met earlier in the book, who decide that they will Spend the Kids' Inheritance, and enjoy the money while they have it. I did actually meet a man once at a party who described himself as a 'Silver Surfer OAP SKIer'. I think he was proud of it, and it certainly made him sound more interesting. He spent an hour and a half recounting his climb up the Wetterhorn and his development of two chalets in Grindelwald.

* Senior Citizens

This term is mainly used by politicians and often preceded by the protective 'our'. 'Our Senior citizens' is used in the same breath as 'our children'; usually signifying that both ends of the age grouping are in need of special help from those in the mainstream of daily life.

It is a patronising but harmless term, and quite meaningless, like most politicians' speeches. When are people 'Junior Citizens', I wonder.

* Saga Lads

This is an affectionate term first used for the enthusiastic travellers with the excellent Saga organisation. Saga, once a lonely player in the over-50 market, has probably done more to enfranchise the generation in their Third Act than any other organisation. They have a selection of services specifically designed for the 50plus group, including an excellent share-buying arm, which I use.

This term often appears in the Press, but sometimes amended to Saga Lout. This usually headlines a story of an older man having Ugandan discussions with a lady not his wife, on the upper deck of a cruise ship in the Caribbean.

* Twirlies

Finally a nickname that is not sociologically important, nor patronising, but was affectionately first used by bus drivers, and is now much used by comedians in their stage shows, who often welcome the Twirlies in their matinee audience.

After you reach 60, railways and coach operators are happy to offer you discounts at certain times, as are museums, cinemas and country houses. In many cities you can also use a Bus Pass to get free bus travel, once you have sneaked quietly into the Post Office, with a couple of passport photos and a rates bill, and got your magic pass.

There are, however, limitations to this act of generosity, and among them is that it is not valid at commuting to work times. Many people are uncertain when this ends, and so they ask, '*Is it too early?*' Said quickly this becomes Twirly, and so the many distinguished users of the Bus Pass are known as Twirlies.

All of these may be fun to the sociologists and the marketeers, but too often have a patronising air. We are not Senior Citizens, which makes us sound like a brand of our parents' cigarettes. Nor are we Old Age Pensioners, OAPs, Oldies, Nifties, 60plusses, 50plusses, or Twirlies.

We cannot be pigeonholed into some generic marketing group, We are engineers, civil servants, financiers, teachers, IT geeks, managers, salesmen, consultants, as mixed a group as any age. We have another 20 good years to use our experience and knowledge to reshape not just our own lives, but also the organisations to whom we contribute. We are not at the end of our careers, but at another beginning.

It seems a particularly strange attitude to a generation, who, in truth, are the most knowledgeable, the richest, and potentially the most powerful political force in the marketplace. They are, after all, trying to pigeonhole a group of the people, who own 80% of the wealth of the country, account for 30% of all consumer expenditure, and deliver nearly 50% of the votes.

Ignore all their condescending put-downs, reject their acronyms, and refuse to be pigeonholed into some meaningless group. If you confess to anything, let it be that you are a Silver Wolf setting out on your new life, and you have this unique Grand Plan to achieve your ambitions and dreams.

QUESTIONS

1. Do you currently see yourself as part of any of these groups?

2. Do you find that others try to pigeonhole you?

3. If they do, will you tell them that you are a Silver Wolf?

CHAPTER 21

"I grow old… I grow old… I shall wear the bottoms of my trousers rolled."

T S Eliot

Between You and Me

Would you prefer to be old?

No, this chapter is not a cop out. I'm not suggesting that you ever want to be old, but I am very aware how easy it could be to fall into 'old' habits, and become old by default.

I am thinking here of a friend, who asked me about *Silver Wolf*. After listening to my going on about using our Third Act and creating a Grand Plan for a new 20-year life style, he quietly said, *"Do I have to make this Grand Plan? I'm looking forward to being old and doing nothing."*

I quickly replied that, of course, he didn't have to change anything; it is his life, and only he will decide what to do with it. All that I was suggesting is that we have a chance to stop the race we'd been running for 30–40 years, reappraise our hopes and dreams, and set about making them happen.

All this in a life where work and play were better balanced, and where we lived to make our dreams come true – or at least some of them – not just to work and pay the mortgage.

I confess to being shocked at first by his attitude, because he had always led a full life as an oil executive, but he was clearly tired and, at the moment we talked, all he wanted was the thought of doing nothing.

And for ten months he became old. He ate too much, watched endless television, napped in the afternoon, and got fat. We were all beginning to worry about him, until one day he rang me up. *"OK,"* he yelled. *"I've done the retirement bit. It's boring. Now, what was it that we have to do?"*

He's now sketched out his life for the next 15 years, has taken a consultancy for 100 days a year with some power company, is learning Italian, writing his memoirs, and looking for some land in Umbria to develop three houses for his and two other families.

I'm glad he's rejoined the world. He was too alive and enthusiastic to have acquired those traits that characterise traditional old people.

Perhaps the saddest thing about those non-members of the Third Act, those who decline to take their chance to have the best years of their lives, is the way they behave. I reckon they all have six main characteristics, and it's almost as if they all went to the same hypnotist, who taught them that, if they want to be old, they must follow these rules.

You, of course, will never follow these rules, but I pass them on as a reminder of how easy it is to fall into the trap of being old. You may think this a little tongue in cheek, but then again, never was a truer word said in jest.

1. You must learn how to be constantly not well. Not ill, just *'not well'*

With nothing to do, you will find that your body begins to fall apart. A little fibrillation of the heart? A weak knee? Bit of a swelling round the ankles? Stomach ache after eating? There will be lots of things to worry about, and build up in your mind.

You'll find yourself seeing the old Doc a bit more, asking for a few tests down at the hospital. What's more, you will look forward to them! You will come to enjoy those monthly visits to the hospital, meeting all those other nice people with their little problems. And it does fill up an interesting morning, with time for a coffee at Starbucks as a treat.

You might even become a sort of paramedic, spreading bits of medical wisdom you've picked up from chatting in the wait at the pharmacy. "*Not that I'm an actual doctor,*" you tell everyone. "*But when you've had as many problems as me, you soon learn your way around the body,*" you add modestly.

Such will become your enthusiasm for your illnesses that you will transform the polite question '*How are you?*' into an invitation to let the whole world know the fascinating story of your twisted big toe. This wasn't, of course, gout, but some strange new disease – probably foreign – that the doctors don't yet know how to fix. *"They've tried breaking it and resetting, but that didn't work."*

With a bit of luck your aches and pains will become the centre of your life, and you will become a martyr to them. You will soon forget how few illnesses are inflicted on those of your contemporaries, who continue to live happy fulfilled lives.

2. You must grumble a great deal

This is an essential characteristic of 'the old'. You must grumble about everything, consistently, interminably, and loudly. Nothing is nearly as good as it was in 'your day,' you tell the world, and illustrate this point about manners, speech, entertainment, sportsmen, politicians, morals, everything.

Of course, you have already given yourself away by talking about 'your day' as if you no longer had a day. Only those who regard their lives as static and finished can live only in the past. Those who are still alive know that their days are continuing, and contemporary.

This won't stop you from grumbling about everything and everyone at every moment of the day.

3. You must talk constantly about the past

Nothing wrong with talking about the past to one's contemporaries. It is a great joy at any age to reminisce with your generation about times in the past, and to relive some of your more glorious moments, even if they did happen more decades ago than you care to remember. It is also a great way to feel young again, to see yourself as that callow youth, climbing that Alpine peak in summer clothes, because you didn't know any better.

Going down Memory Lane is a great pleasure in life, and we all do it. But not all the time, and certainly not to those who weren't alive then. Those determined to be 'old' forget this caveat, and go on endlessly about their past, which, of course, was always better. The sun shone all summer, love was simple and pure, God was in his Heaven, and all was right with the world.

And, as we hobbled the ten miles to school, scrumping an

apple from the orchard, because there was no food at home, we sang arias from The Messiah. Oh yes, oh yes.

If your past is really interesting, then you may have some in your family, who will happily indulge you, but most people will, sadly, only put on that patronising response that they adopt solely for those they regard as 'old'.

4. You must dislike the young

The 'old' dislike the young. They hate their lack of respect and deference; they envy them their strength; they fear their confidence. They have already decided that they are at war with the world, and the world, of course, belongs to the young. So, the young are their natural enemies.

They start off disliking the generation behind them, the ones they blame for taking their jobs, the ones who shed crocodile tears when they left. They soon move down the scale and turn against those starting off their families, who haul their noisy brats around with them, so there's no peace anywhere.

Soon they concentrate their dislike onto 'the young', the generation they really don't begin to understand, all of whom are yobs in their eyes. Before long they end up hating anyone younger than themselves.

They often try to exclude their own grandchildren from this dislike, but, even there, some of them privately confess to their cronies that they'd prefer to live in a world where the young were seen and not heard. Preferably not even seen for more than an hour at a time.

The worst thing is that they soon become convinced that all 'young' people believe all 'old' people are worthless. They, of course, have long convinced themselves that all young people certainly are.

5. You should walk with a stoop

This is the true sign of the 'old'. When you have acquired that traditional stoop, you will have managed to send a clear call to the world that you have joined the ranks of the 'old'.

There are a number of explanations for this stoop. The kindest of these is that you have back pain, and bending over seems to help it. It is true that most of us have some back pain that usually starts in our forties, and wear and tear doesn't help that ache at the base of the spine. But bending over does not help it: sitting sensibly will do far more good.

Psychologists sometimes say that it is an unconscious expression of avoiding the world. They are often accused of saying anything that sounds profound, and which will earn them giant fees, but their view is that you lean over to avoid contact with the world around you.

You may laugh at this, but think about it. Why do the 'old' so often bend? Are they in pain? Are they in such a hurry that they lower their head to walk faster, because they have so much to do? Or are the quacks right, and they just no longer want to see the people and things around them?

Whatever the reason, it is seen as a sign of submission that you can no longer hold your head high and proud. Big John Wayne never stooped, even when cancer was eating him away; so why would you?

6. Don't forget to become forgetful

This is an affectation used by all those who decide to be 'old'. It is one of the eternal myths about age, that it diminishes the memory. Which it does. Every year, starting certainly by the age of 30.

Nevertheless, now that they are going to be 'old', they can really use this myth. They can become, as they see it, that lovingly eccentric old person, who keeps on having 'senior moments', and forgets where their glasses are.

Glasses are a good example. Keys can provide some good moments of panic; as can forgetting credit cards, bag and mobile. An out of date passport at the airport adds to the drama of travel.

This affectation of forgetfulness can be mildly amusing to those around them at first, but becomes increasingly annoying. Those who allow it to continue, often find that they become genuinely forgetful, not because they have too much to remember, but too little. Let the mind die, and it will turn this idiosyncrasy into a real problem.

They refuse to use lists, because they think it makes them old. Nonsense. Have a look around your supermarket. Most people are carrying lists, they are under forty, and still can't finish their shopping without checking with someone on the mobile.

And, didn't we all make lists all your life? What are contact reports of meetings but lists? What are strategic plans but lists? What is our computer address book but a list? Didn't we write down new instructions for getting to a new place when we were 40? So what's different now?

Still, for those who decide to become forgetful, the car is where they can really display this to the world. A real 'old' person can litter their car with Post-its. *Check the Lights. Turn off Radio. I live at...... My Telephone Number is....3rd round-about to supermarket.* And so on. A friend of my father's had eight, which included, rather worryingly, *Brake on left* and *Red means stop.*

I know that anyone typifying all these six points might seem a caricature, but that is the image that our parents often presented to the world, giving a distinctive character to what the world thought of as 'old'.

By seeing themselves as 'old', many fell into the trap of conforming to this caricature, and so were treated differently by the rest of the world, and made an easy target for ageism.

It is a perfectly reasonable view to take, that we *are* getting older, our bodies need just that bit more care than 30 years ago, our appearance *has* changed, so forget the whole rotten world – which is going to hell anyhow – and let's shuffle along to the end.

It's easy to mock those who do this, but it is very easy some days to join them. There comes a day when you just don't want to fight any more. You don't want to work. You don't want to keep your body fit. You don't want to start the day with the crossword.

You don't want to see the children and even less the noisy grandchildren. You don't want to do your consultancy/autobi-ography/painting/garden/charity work. You don't want to involve yourself in some great political debate of the day.

To be honest, you don't actually want to do anything.

We all have those self-pitying, self-indulgent days, and we have to remind ourselves that we actually had these moments in every past decade, and that they are not the prerogative of those in the Third Act.

Most of us have probably cried out in frustration, '*I hate the world, what's the point of living?*' long before we reached anything approaching middle-age. So, it isn't any moment of great significance, just a letting off of steam.

Forget that moment and immediately start planning a new project, which will remind us of why we had The Great Plan to achieve our dreams,

To those who decide to be 'old', I say fine, but you may find life more enjoyable if you avoid some of these habits handed down from the previous generation. They only confirm the image of us as a species apart, and this doesn't help those of us, who have no intention of growing old, gracefully or disgracefully.

The most important point, surely, is that those who do decide to be old are missing out on the chance of a lifetime, the best chance, for some, to make sense of their life. We've done our duty, we've worked our shift – use any cliché you like – now we have these 20 years to make a paradise down here on earth, when we can achieve some of our dreams. For goodness sake, haven't we earned it now? Being 'old' seems like a pretty poor alternative.

QUESTIONS

1. Do *you* ever want to be 'old'?

2. Do you detect any of these 'old' affectations in any of your contemporaries?

3. How were your parents 'old'?

CHAPTER 22

"In my experience there's no such thing as luck."
Obi-Wan Kenobi

May the Force Be with You

We have the votes. Now let's use them. These Ten Commitments in the next Prime Minister's Manifesto will do for a start

This chapter is about our political power. The political power that could be used by those of us in our Third Act, who now make up the largest political group in the country. We are what is called in political circles the Grey Vote, and currently not high on any Party's agenda. This will now change.

Politicians still make the mistake of thinking they can buy us off cheaply. Even at the 2005 election they thought that throwing a few scraps of pounds for winter fuel, or free TV after 75 would do it. Those bribes reflected their dismissive attitude to us, as being easy to bribe, but not worth bothering too much about.

By 2009, they will have to bother about us. Because, by then, we could easily make up over 50% of the votes cast. Without our votes no Party can ever again hope to be elected. It's time for us to band together, and remind all MPs in Westminster that we are the largest lobby group in the country, and that there are a few things we'd like changed.

What I am suggesting here is that we use our voting power to make certain that any aspiring political leader of the future has to have us on board.

Am I overdoing our potential power? I reckon there are three basic reasons why not. We have three things going for us.

We are plentiful. We vote. We are rich.

- **We are plentiful**. Half the households in the UK are headed by someone over 55. Not a bad start. There are some 20 million of us over 55. Even if only half start lobbying, there are still a lot of us.

- **We vote**. We still believe in the old-fashioned view that democracy has no meaning if citizens don't vote. Fortunately for us, but unfortunately for democracy, the younger generation seems to take democracy for granted, and only a few bother to vote.

  At the last election only some 40% of the 18–34 voted; nearly 70% of us did. There are 46 million people empowered to vote. In 2005 some 27 million actually voted; of those, we accounted for nearly 12 million.

  By the next election, for the first time in the history of British democracy, those over 50 will hold the casting vote. Think on it.

- **We are rich**. Political Parties live off gifts from rich people and companies, and that means us. We're not all rich by any means, but a chunk of us are. I see a potential Trojan scenario here. Those good ladies famously withdrew their nightly favours until their men agreed to their requests.

  I suggest that we withdraw our donations to any Party that is not committed to the changes that we seek.

What do we want in return for our vote? Of course, we want to get back to those much-mocked old-fashioned values. We want to return to some of those standards that have been swept away in the rush to a dumbed-down society.

There are dozens of national changes that we want, but first of all we need to lobby for practical changes on things that will affect our Third Act lives. Work, Pensions and Ageism.

Above all, we need a political leader who understands the harm that ageism brought to millions, the stupidity of many of the restrictive tax and pension regulations, and the need to harness a work force from every age.

Ageism, like racism and sexism, is a subtle underbelly to our Third Act. The obsession with Youth, which many of us happily fostered in the Sixties, has rebounded on us. What we meant to happen was to persuade the grown-up world to allow us, while still young, to play a more exciting part in the working life.

What has happened is that, by some curious form of osmosis, the world has persuaded itself that to be young is the only thing of importance in the work place. We have to ensure that the EU ruling on Age Discrimination is supported by the Government in more than just words.

As a start, I am including here a draft speech for the next political leader who wants to run the country.

There's probably little new in it to you as a Silver Wolf, but I've never heard it from the lips of a politician. Adapt and change it as you think fit, but send your version to your local MP as a start, so that he knows what you want, if he wants your vote next time.

DRAFT SPEECH FOR THE LEADER OF ANY PARTY
WISHING TO BECOME THE NEXT PRIME MINISTER

THE END OF AGEISM

Today I want to talk about an injustice that should be ended. It is an injustice that has been seeping into our social system and attitudes for too many decades. It is an injustice that I and my Party intend to end.

I am talking about Ageism. The attitude that condemned people in the prime of their life to early unemployment. The attitude that presumed anyone over 50 to be over the hill. The attitude that, in previous decades, has set aside a third of our adult population, as if they were not worthy of our attention.

You and I both know that ageism has been illegal since the Act of the European Union imposed this on all member states. In this country it came into force in October 2006. But you and I also know that it hasn't yet had a large enough effect.

We've all lived through the battles to end Racism. We may not have won that battle yet, but we are winning it. We have all lived through the battles to end Sexism. There is still much to be done, but, as Margaret Thatcher showed, a woman can now become not only Head of State, but also Head of Government.

Ageism, however, in spite of the Age Discrimination Act, is still alive. In some businesses, people are still regarded as getting too old to be of further value, once they pass 50, even though the new law forbids them to be sacked on grounds of age.

I understand why companies attempt to become leaner organisations, but why do some of them throw out the people with the most experience, and whose ages match those of many of the company's clients?

The answer, I'm afraid, is the hangover from ageism, an attitude born from a heap of myths, none of which are true. There is the myth that we become stupider, because we lose so many brain cells every year of our lives. It is not true. **Even at the grand age of 70, we have only lost 3% of the brain's cells.**

The second myth says that you can't teach an old dog new tricks. So there is no point in sending older people to retraining courses. Nonsense. **The ability to learn is as great at 55 as it was at 25. Parts of our minds are weaker; parts stronger. But the total ability is the same.**

The new Act now makes training open to all workers, without any age discrimination, but the result of the old ageism is that we still have an almost secret army of unemployed. **We do not have one million unemployed in this country; we have nearer five million.** Because nearly four million people over 50 who want to work, or who may need to work, are without a fulltime job.

The change in the workplace is dramatic. **Fifty years ago nearly everyone in the age group of 50–65 was working full-time. Today it is less than 70%.** Of people over 65 years, one in three were still working 50 years ago. Today less than one in ten work full, or even part, time.

But surely that's a good thing, say some, trying to justify this wholesale sacking of a generation. It means that people have a longer retirement. Which of course they do, and many, especially those in jobs that require hard physical work, are often happy to stop early. **But here we come to another myth, the myth that Retirement is the gateway to eternal happiness. Alas that is rarely true.**

Retirement is often a joyous period for a while, and this pleasure usually lasts, according to the sociologists, for anything up to a year. Then many find that, by opting out of work, they feel they have opted out of life. They begin to feel isolated from the central community, and gradually many feel alienated from the main stream of society.

Of course, this is not true of all retired people. Many have enough money to fill their lives with the pleasures they saved hard for over the decades. Many find satisfaction in giving their time and talents to voluntary work.

But the majority do not want to stop work entirely. They would like to work, if only part-time. They would like to continue as part of the normal life. **Many have come to realise that we are essentially working and social animals. We need the contacts with colleagues, as much as with our own family and friends.**

Millions more want to work, because they need to earn a little more income. I'm not talking here only about people who never saved for their later years. I'm talking about those who did save, but have found their dream not as golden as the salesman told them. Lower annuity rates and a weak stock market have produced personal pensions far lower than anticipated, and certainly too little income to last another 20 years.

Twenty years. More for some. **This is the crux of the challenge. Our so-called Retirement is no longer for a few years. It is for a life span longer than that of childhood.**

The official Life Expectancy now is that, at 50, we are expected to reach 77 years. At 60 we will reach 79 years. At 65 we'll make a further two years to 81.

All this is a far cry from a century ago when the whole idea of retirement began. No one in the history of the world had ever before lived in a society that decided when a person should stop work. Then, nearly 100 years ago, the Government of the day said that people should retire at 70, and would receive a pension from the State for their long years of productivity.

Why 70? Was it because we all become senile after that, or were incapable of great work? A quick look at the great men of history, from Leonardo da Vinci to Bertrand Russell, would confirm the answer to be No.

The truth is that the average age of death in those days was 69, and the Government thought it had enough money in the pension box to pay out to the few who lived a year longer.

Don't mock those well-intentioned Liberals of the day. The State pension box today is still short of a few billion that will have to be found, if we are all going to live for so many more years. Nor, by the way, is the state pension much larger today.

What we do with these years is clearly up to each of us individually, but what I have come to realise is that many things have to change. People of all ages must have the chance to work if they wish or need to, to realise their assets if they wish to, and not to be penalised if they do wish to work.

This is why I am pledging today, to the millions who may still be suffering from age-related injustices, that my Government will campaign against ageism in every form, and will remove some of the financial disincentives to saving for and working into our later years.

My 10 Point Pledge

1. Any Government of mine will work closely with the representatives of all sides in industry, to ensure that Age Discrimination is ended not just in word, but in action.

2. We will stress that the retention of older people in the workplace will not only benefit them, but also the company balance sheet. We will campaign for flexi-working in both the private and public sectors.

   There is nothing sacred about a five-day week for everyone. Where possible, people should be allowed to work four or three-day weeks, so that they can continue to play a part in the work force, but also have more time for their other pursuits.

3. We will remove any anomalies of taxation on personal pensions and on company pension rules that are a disincentive to those who wish to continue to work.

4. We will commit to the return of the State Pension to increase annually in line with the average earnings increase.

5. We will abolish any fixed retirement age below 70.

6. We will extend the earnings allowance for those over 69 to £10,000.

7. We will abolish taxation on the first £5,000 of any pension income.

8. We will investigate the complexities of social security benefits and produce a code understandable to all.

9. We will plan to raise the age from which state employees' pensions may be taken to 60.

10. On housing, we will explore all ways to help millions who are currently what is sometimes called Asset Rich and Cash Poor. The country needs more of those assets to be released onto the market, as much as property owners need to release them for their own plans.

I am not suggesting that money is going to solve the challenges of this New Age. Money is important to all of us, but, far more important, is the change of attitudes, not only about older people, but also by those people.

As a society we have to realise, and as individuals we must understand, that the old pattern of our lives has gone. It is no longer 20 years education, 45 years work, 5 years retirement, and goodnight. It is currently more likely to be 20 years education, 35 to 40 years work, and 20 to 25 years of a third life.

What will we do with these 20 years? That is our challenge both as individuals and as a nation. I don't pretend to have all the answers to this challenge. But I think it is the duty of anyone asking for your trust to run this country, to open up a debate on some of these major challenges that will affect our future lives.

What I do know is that the 20 million people, a third of the country, the Silver Wolves, as they have been called, now in their Third Act, deserve a society that appreciates their worth, respects their knowledge, and welcomes their contribution.

END

CHAPTER 23

"Which were my happiest years? Always the ones to come."

Bernard Berenson

The Happiest Years of Your Life

The 10 things always to remember

The aim of *Silver Wolf* is that the twenty or more years of your Third Act should be the best years of your life. I have tried in these pages to suggest what you need to do, to give yourself a wonderfully happy Third Act, when you create a new balance of your life between working, learning and fulfilling your dreams.

I have suggested that you need to remember ten things above all others that are fundamental to your happiness. They have all been discussed in previous chapters, but here is a brief final reminder.

1. **It's all in your mind**

   Get out of your head any of the old myths about getting older. No single age automatically brings any dramatic change to your mind or body; nor do you ever become less capable of working, learning, creating and playing a full role in life.

   Remember that getting older successfully is all in the mind.

   You are as young as you look, as young as you behave, and as young as you believe yourself to be. Be conscious of your appearance; stay interested in the world; and don't fall into any of the old habits that infested many of our parents.

   You are not retiring from life, as so many of them did, you are starting out on a new life.

2. **Keep working**

    Work is paramount to your success. You don't want to work full-time, but you do need to work some of the time. All play and no work makes Jack a very dull boy. Never think of Retiring; that was an aberration that never worked.

    You need to continue to work for many reasons. You are a social being and need the relationship with others of all ages. You are a hunter and need to bring something back from the hills. You need workdays to sharpen the pleasure of your play days; without them, play days can quickly seem like work.

    Even if you have no financial need to work, still keep working at something for some of the time. Work is important to your status, your self-perception, your contribution to society – and the enjoyment of your other plans.

3. **Decide how you will achieve your dreams**

    You've worked full time for 35 years, you've brought up a family, bought a home and survived the rat race with only a few bruises. Now the children are leaving home, the mortgage payments ending, and your world is changing.

    This is the time to remember all the dreams and ambitions that got forgotten in the long working days. It is more than that; now is the time to fulfil those dreams and realise those ambitions.

    The Third Act is when you do what you always wanted to do, and become what you always meant to be. It is about achieving these aims, and becoming happier than you ever have been.

4. **Make your Grand Plan**

    Your happiness for the next 20 years deserves some planning, and it is so important that you need a Grand Plan. This Grand Plan is how you see your next two decades, what you plan to achieve, what work you intend to do, what you hope to learn, what fun you intend to have, what lifestyle you wish to enjoy.

    It is the blueprint for your happiness to take you into your late seventies. You will want to ask yourself a lot of questions, and be totally honest with your answers. Your Grand Plan is more important than any proposals you ever wrote for anyone else; this is your life. Don't rush it.

5. **Surround yourself with love**

Before you can begin on the great adventure into your Third Act, you need to be certain that your partner, children, parents and friends are with you. No one is more important than your partner, because, without a loving home, your achievements can often seem hollow.

You will need her love and support, just as she will need yours in fulfilling her own dreams for these years. You will need the love and understanding of your children; you will want to enjoy the affection and friendship of old chums, who have their own agendas. Dismiss the miserable ones; they have already lost the plot.

With all those around you, sort out any old differences, clear up any misunderstandings, forget old hurts. You are starting again, and need no unhappiness lingering over from the past. Nothing is more important to your enjoyment of the next decade than to live it within a loving world.

6. **Do your sums**

Are you certain how much savings you have, what your investments are worth, how much you spend a year in basic living, and how much income you receive? And do you know how much you will need as the cost of living grows?

If you're like I was, all the answers are NO. But you have to know your financial situation, if you are going to achieve your dreams. The Third Act is no time for financial crises, and you need to have as clear an idea of your future finances as you do of your ambitions.

Feed all your figures into Excel, stir for inflation, leave to simmer for a month, and see what you've missed out. If the final result reveals a slight hiccup in cash flow at any time – as it does for most of us – work out how to cover it.

The unending success of the Grand Plan may depend on your skill as a financial controller.

7. **Keep fit**

If you're planning to have the best years of your life, there's little point in living the kind of life that is programmed to bring on more illness and an earlier death. One thing the years do bring us is a small loss of physical strength each year, and your body needs more cherishing after 50 than before.

Look after your body and it will look after you. You want to postpone getting any illness for as late as possible, as medical knowledge doubles every three years, and hopes even to control cancer within 20 years. Eating sensibly, drinking modestly and exercising daily is a good start.

8. **Make your home work for you**

Your home is the centre of both your personal and financial life in your Third Act. Your children will be there less, but you will be there more. If you stay in your existing home, make it work for you, laid out the way you want, in the colours you want, giving the atmosphere that is right for your new life.

If you need more money, then make it work for you by raising loans against it to fund your new business plans or personal dreams. Your home has probably been your best investment in the past; now it can become both your HQ and your treasury.

9. **Smile**

Be optimistic. Be positive. Be happy. Smile. You are lucky to have the chance of a longer life, a better life, a healthy life, but it is all pointless if you don't acknowledge your luck and live it to the full.

From now on the glass is always half full, the sun is always about to shine, and anything is possible. You are delighted to be alive, and excited at embarking on your new life. Many of us forgot how to smile in those heavy fulltime working years; now is the time to remember and greet the world each day with a smile.

10. **Be Yourself**

This is not the time for putting on an act, which was often

necessary during the previous decades. It is time for you to be yourself, be honest with what you want to be, what you want to do, and what you want to achieve. This is no rehearsal; this is the Act when you leave your mark.

All clichés? Of course, but that's the trouble with clichés, they're usually true. Good luck in making these particular clichés come true again for you.

QUESTIONS

1. Which of these 10 points are the most relevant to you?

2. Are there more important points that you think should be included?

3. Will you have any difficulty in following any of the points?

CHAPTER 24

"People never grow old who stand, like curious children, before the great mystery, into which we were born."

Albert Einstein

Last Word

So, Silver Wolf, it's now up to you

Here we are at the end of the book, and the end of the theory. It is now up to you to put into practice whichever parts of the book you found relevant to your life. I hope that most of it has helped you to look forward to your future with confidence and the knowledge that the best years are to come.

Above all, I hope that you now realise that most of the myths about age are just that – myths and not true. Life does not end in your fifties; a new life begins.

What I have suggested in *Silver Wolf* is very simple, but could change your life. The suggestion is that you replan your life at some time in your fifties to create a Third Act, in which you can achieve the dreams and enjoy the pleasures that you always wanted.

It really doesn't matter what those ambitions and dreams are. It doesn't matter if they are modest or extravagant, they are what you want, and, by achieving these, you might make the next 20 years the happiest of your life.

I have stressed in all chapters that you are the only one who can change your life. You now finally take control of your life, and decide what it is you want from the next 20 years.

I have suggested that, before you begin your Third Act, you will want to ask yourself a lot of questions. Your answers to these will clarify your priorities and enable you to make a Grand Plan for the next decade or two.

I have given the plan this grandiose description, because it is such an important moment in your life. For many of us it is both the first and the last Plan that we will draw up for our own happiness and fulfilment. It becomes the blueprint for the rest of your life.

I have argued that we are at the beginning of a social revolution, which will bring changes in almost every aspect of modern living. You are privileged to be able to enjoy a long Third Act that is unique to any generation. Never before in the known history of the world has any generation been given such an opportunity to make a completely new life.

You are part of the first generation, which can expect to live at least to 80. You can also expect to lead a perfectly normal healthy life. It is not just that you will live longer; you can also expect a decent quality of life.

You also reach your Third Act at a time when Ageism becomes illegal. The working world is changing its attitude, and needs your experience and knowledge. More and more companies now accept that most of you will want only to work part-time, and are changing their structure to accommodate you.

You can continue to work, but as part of your new balance of work and personal life, and not the dominating part of your life. This new balance should provide the best years of your life.

It is, in corporate speak, a window of opportunity. You can choose to do nothing of any significance, as many of our parents chose, and accept their myths of ageism.

Or, you can start a new life.

This is why I have suggested in *Silver Wolf* that there has never been a better time to be over 50.

In *Silver Wolf* I have constantly stressed that, as a healthy long age is now likely for most of us, retirement, in the old sense, is no longer even an option, when so much can still be achieved. Retirement may work as an epilogue in your late seventies or early eighties, but never for the 20 years of your Third Act.

No one, and no book, can tell you what your Grand Plan should be. Only you can do that. It is you who identify the goals; you who lay down the timetable; you who establish the priorities; and you who prepare the financial base, upon which your plan can survive.

Dreams often got lost in the race for promotion, to earn the money to pay off the mortgage and bring up the family. But you have done that, and have earned the right to move on. Now is the time to fulfil those dreams.

I hope this book, dedicated to all Silver Wolves, has been of some help. Your life, is no longer a rehearsal; this is it. So take this book and use it to start a new, brilliant chapter in your life.

AND FINALLY...

I hope you have enjoyed reading *Silver Wolf*, and have found it useful in making your Grand Plan for your Third Act.

For the next edition, I would like to include some case histories from readers, who have realised that life now has another 20 years of happiness, and have made their own Grand Plans for making the most of this time.

It doesn't matter whether you choose to continue in the same job, become a SKI-er, go back to university, write a book, start a new family, travel to Peru, move to Spain or set up your own company. All your Third Act scenarios would be welcomed.

Please email me your story, using a *nom de plume* if you prefer, and keeping it to no more than 300 words. Send all case histories to me at *petercarvell@silver-wolf.co.uk*.

I also would like to add a Resources Appendix on services and products that you found helpful in carrying out your Grand Plan. So many readers have already requested help in every aspect of their Grand Plan, and your experience will help others who come after you.

Again please send any recommendations to *petercarvell@silver-wolf.co.uk*.

"When you stop asking questions, you start to die."
Albert Einstein

Some Questions

I hope by now that you have the answers to the 30 questions that I am most often asked. If you are still uncertain about any part of this book, please send me an email to *petercarvell@silver-wolf.co.uk.*

1. Why do you use the term *Silver Wolf*?

2. What do you want the readers of *Silver Wolf* actually to do?

3. Why should they want to do all that?

4. Can this Third Act start sooner than the fifties?

5. Is it too late to start the Third Act in your sixties?

6. I understand the concept of the Grand Plan, but how do I actually begin to do it?

7. Why does it take so long?

8. What are these dreams that you hope readers can fulfil in what you call their Third Act?

9. A 20-year Grand Plan sounds good, but how do I know my money will last?

10. If I have enough money, do I still need to work?

11. Do you really believe we should keep on working until we drop and never retire?

12. Are all the old myths of ageing now found to be false?

13. Do people's memories get worse?

14. Do you really believe that the Age Discrimination Act will change everything?

15. But isn't it true that the older we get, the less we are capable of being retrained?

16. But it must be true that the older we get, the more we are ill, surely?

17. Is it too late to change any bad eating and drinking habits?

18. Are you serious about needing to change the way we look?

19. Is sex really so important?

20. Should people change homes in their Third Act?

21. Does a home in the sun make sense?

22. Is equity release a wrong way of raising money from the home?

23. Do I have to save money for the children?

24. Do you really believe that we can become a political force?

25. Should we lie about our age?

26. Is there a Pension Crisis?

27. Can we do anything practical about our pensions now?

28. Should we consider Buy to Let property investments?

29. Your book was written with men in mind. Isn't it a guide also for women?

30. Do I really *have* to make a Grand Plan for myself?

"I'm as young as my cosmetic surgeon can make me."
Joan Rivers

A Cut in Time

Are you ready for cosmetic surgery?

Would you have your face lifted? I had never considered it, but now have to confess that I did succumb to the temptation for a minor adjustment. It happened partly for reasons of vanity, partly a journalistic desire to know what actually goes on, but mainly because I had just had a lucky play in the stock market, on the same day as I met a cosmetic surgeon at a dinner party.

"In 10 years, millions in their 50s and 60s will have cosmetic surgery. It is already a boom industry in America, but this is spreading to Europe, as people come to realise that they need not look old, if they don't want to" he told me.

"The new older generation will not accept the physical changes that old age used to bring, but will want to prolong their youthful appearance and attitudes."

In a moment of impetuosity I decided to see a man about a cut in time. The actual surgery was a strange experience, a bit like being allowed into a secret society where the rituals are new, but all acolytes are welcomed. Was it a painful experience? No. Was it horrifically expensive? No. Did it change the way I look? Yes, but only because it took me back to the way I used to look, rather than the man with two inches too much skin hanging round the face. Will it last? Not forever, but hopefully ten years.

Would I recommend it? It depends on how important the way you look is to you, but Yes, I now would.

I kept a diary of the moment of truth, and here it is, for any of you who might be afflicted with the same desire to push back the years, and have wondered what it would be like.

THE START

Am I mad? Why have I just booked an appointment to see a cosmetic surgeon? I have a list of reasons that made me make the call.

- I'm beginning to look old. The body may be reasonable still, but the face is dropping in two slight jowls, and the jaw line on one side sits on a turkey gobble.

- So what? What's wrong with looking 60 plus? Absolutely nothing, but I have no intention of leaving the world of work for another 10–15 years, and don't want to be an easy victim of ageism. So long as ageism lives, however illegally, we need all the help we can get, and that includes the way we look.

- Two people in the last few months have suggested that I look miserable. I know why. It's because the corners of my mouth now turn down. Unless I walk along with a perpetual smile, I realise that I must look miserable.

- I don't like the way I look. Here's the vanity bit. I can look acceptable in the right light and at the right angle, and that's what I see when I'm shaving. Then last month a friend took some pictures in the garden that caught me in the wrong light and at the wrong angle and I saw how I really looked.

- So, alright then, it comes down to vanity in the end, but vanity with a purpose. To look happy, to look more like I always was. That's the key, I suppose. I just want to look the way I used to look for decades.

A WEEK LATER

Saw the cosmetic surgeon today. He has rooms in Harley Street, not exactly the best in the house, but he was terrific. My wife, who came with me, thought he was the most devastatingly good-looking man she'd met in ages.

His name is Dr Badiali, an Italian, who spoke fluent English and French, looks like a young Marcello Mastroianni, and works at several clinics in three countries, including the Elyzea in Brussels.

"*Tell me what you want,*" was his opener. So I told him all the points I'd put down last week. He pulled at the skin on my face, showing what he could do, and suggested an S-Lift, and a little liposuction on the neck. He didn't like doing a full face lift, on men, as it can easily make the face look unnatural,

The reason for his first question was that he wanted to know my expectations. Too many people turn to cosmetic surgery with unreal expectations, he said, and so he likes to establish at the beginning what can be done.

The operation apparently lasts around two hours, followed by some six hours in the Recovery Room, and then I could either stay in the clinic or go to the hotel. Whichever I chose, he would want to see me next day to check my face and bandages. He would then replace them, and add a kind of hood, which goes round the head and under the neck. This I would have to wear all day and night for seven days.

What about pain? Usually very little with an S-Lift. I would probably want to stay at home for at least three days afterwards, as that first period needs rest.

Am I badly swollen? Not necessarily, but your face will be bruised and swollen, he said, and you need to help it with ice and arnica tablets.

When could I go back to work? Certainly, at the end of a fortnight, maybe earlier.

NEXT DAY

Have been thinking about yesterday's consultation. I liked him enormously. He didn't turn it into a great drama; he was clear on what could be done by cosmetic surgery; he listened to what I wanted, and answered every question.

Funny game, cosmetic surgery. Full of hype and conflicting stories, and there's no easy way to choose your surgeon. Here you are, about to pay someone to cut your face open, and you've really little evidence how well they can actually do the job.

All you can go on is that he has had the right training, that he belongs to the right medical organisations, like the British Association of Aesthetic Plastic Surgeons, and that he's done your op enough times to have a fair chance of getting it right. It really is a secret society, and there are no published guides to check the validity of any particular surgeon's ability and track record.

It's the same with the clinic, I suppose. I checked out some in London, but their prices were higher than my win on Shell. I'd fixed that as the budget, and didn't want any accusations of raiding the family vault.

I checked others in Lille, Brussels, Cracow, Strasbourg, and Amsterdam, but in the end I decided that, if I take this great step for mankind, it will be at the Elyzea Clinic in Brussels. Dr. Badioli would happily do me in London, but it would cost nearly £5,000. In Brussels it will cost under £2,000.

Obviously I asked if this would be a half price job; but he said that was the normal price anywhere in Europe. He could do me in Rome or Amsterdam, Berlin or Barcelona for a similar price; it was only London that cost twice as much.

WEEK LATER

Bit of an anticlimax. The Clinic is booked months ahead, and could only fit me in on October 14th. So now I have 12 weeks to wait. I looked again at their web site, to remind myself of what will then happen. "*The surgeon makes an incision above the hair line at the temples, just above the ear. The face is tightened to produce a natural rejuvenation. Sagging cheeks or jowls can be removed by way of micro-liposculpture*". I feel sick.

Then comes the promise. "*The rejuvenating effect of a mini facelift is truly fantastic. The effect of surgery lasts for about ten years.*" I feel better.

Then comes the warning. *"Although the procedure makes you look 8–10 years younger in a few hours, it cannot completely restore the face you once had, because it is not only your skin and muscles that change with age, but also the bone structure, which is not affected by the surgery."*

A bit of a downer, but at least it's honest. If they get it right on the night, then it will take 10 years off my life and should last for another ten years. I'll buy that.

TEN WEEKS LATER

Operation Facelift begins today. In fact, I suppose it began after the decision was made, because I started moistening my face every night. Dr. Badiali made such a point about the quality of the skin being a key factor in the success of facial surgery that I've been raiding my wife's bathroom shelves for the stuff.

Today is 10 days before the op and I am to cease taking any aspirin, nurofen, or Vitamin E tablets during this period, but they do recommend arnica tablets, which are supposed to help reduce the bruising.

Do I still want to go through with this? The truth is that I do. Am I going to tell anyone? I think not. Much better that family, friends and colleagues just think how much better I'm looking and put it down to the fortnight away.

There is an argument that you should look like your generation, and not change. That seems to me to be nonsense. No generation has just one look. Some people of 60 look 50, some look 70. I'd just prefer to be with the former.

What I don't want is to remain as I've now become. Appearance is always important, and even more so, as you get older, if only because most of us suffer from the one Great Truth of ageing– your face drops a couple of inches between 30 and 60.

The European price, of course, makes my decision easier. As my wife pointed out, the cost was only what the garage had charged for a major service and some new parts for the car last March.

NINE DAYS LATER

Tomorrow is the great day. My wife has organised it like a military operation. She has tried to prepare everything at home, so that, when we return from Brussels, I can disappear from the world. The house is filled with instant food and drink, the refrigerator is stocked with frozen peas and easy-to-eat food.

We take the Eurostar to Brussels, and the Hotel Monty, a few hundred yards from the clinic, is booked.

THE GREAT DAY

I write this as I sit outside the Operating room in the clinic. I'm on at 11.00, with the very charming Dr Ariann Neuprez. She went over the notes I'd made on what I wanted, and the photos, taken in the garden two months ago, that showed me full face and profiles, so that she could see exactly where all my problems were.

Photos help the surgeon enormously, apparently, and this morning she took her own photographs of my face at four angles, and made pen marks, indicating where she would cut.

The anaesthetist promised I would feel nothing, checked my weight and blood pressure, and told me there was nothing to worry about. The op would probably take just over 100 minutes, I would be in a twilight zone, feeling nothing, but not under general anaesthetic, and he promised there shouldn't even be much pain afterwards. He was very reassuring

That's the situation, as I sit here at 10.45. I'm truly not worried about a thing. After all, it's a routine operation, I asked for it to be done, I have no illness, and now apparently it won't even hurt!

Christine, a wonderful motherly smiling nurse, has just summoned me into the OR. Now it's for real.

OP + TWO DAYS

We are now on the Eurostar train returning to London, and I have no idea if it is a success or not. What I had failed to take in was that the black head support goes on immediately after the surgery, so that I will not see my face for another week, when the bandages are removed.

The mask wraps round the face, rather like a scuba diver's kit, leaving just the forehead, eyes and mouth open to view. It will now stay on for two weeks, one week night and day, second week in the night only. The idea is that this gives support to the uplifted face, helping the stitches keep it in place.

I stayed there the night, as I had a couple of drains, but yesterday morning Dr. Badiali had returned, and took a look at Dr Neuprez' work. "*Perfect*" was his view, as he took out the drains, and he promised me I would be very pleased at the result.

Obviously, there was some discomfort, but the clinic doesn't believe in suffering, and supply a selection of painkillers, which have the added virtue of helping you sleep, in addition to the antibiotics. The clinic sees sleep and rest in the first 48 hours as the best cure for the body.

So far I can see, no bruising or discolouration. The face is obviously swollen, but how much I can't tell. The stitches are around the ears, back and front, and I have no feeling there at all. I can't shave until the bandages are off, and even then not where the stitches are; equally no washing the hair until then.

Eating is a slight problem, as they advise you not to chew too hard for the first week, so as not to dislodge any stitches. Also, with that scuba face mask, your mouth cannot open too far. But this really isn't a problem; just cut any food up into small portions, and take a long time chewing – which is exactly what the dieticians tell us to do anyhow.

Today, in the hotel, I did eat a hearty breakfast of coffee, fruit juice, brioche with cheese, and croissant with cherry jam. Breakfast was served at a baronial table for twelve people from five different nations – German, Dutch, Belgian, British and one very elegant Nigerian. No one stared at my exotic headware; just one man asked "*Une bataille avec le dentiste?*" I nodded. It didn't seem the right time and place to open a discussion on rejuvenation.

On the train no one stared; no one asked anything. It was either British reserve or they thought I was a hoodie and best left alone!

OP + FIVE DAYS

Back in the house, and very glad to stay here for a few days. There's still no pain, but I feel pretty stupid, sitting in the chair reading, with two packs of ice over the mask on either side of my face! Still the swelling is going down fast and it's no big deal.

They don't make a big deal about cosmetic surgery in Europe, and that's the right attitude. Obviously some operations are much more serious than mine, but I'm glad to have stayed in Brussels two nights. It would have been perfectly possible to have taken the train home next day, but the full day's rest near the clinic was a kind of insurance, just in case I was one of the 2% who do have a problem after surgery.

OP + EIGHT DAYS

Have just returned from Dr. Badiali in Harley Street. This was the great moment, when my face was finally uncovered after a week of being hidden by that mask. He unwrapped the bandages, swabbed my ears and neck, and said, "*Have a look.*"

The face was a little swollen, and slightly bruised, but the change was actually quite dramatic. I now have a strong jaw line again, the neck is free of that lump, and my cheek bones show more clearly.

The really good news is that the skin has not been drawn back too tightly, in that ghastly way that you see even on Hollywood stars like Michael Douglas, Mickey Rourke, or William Shatner, the gallant captain of 'Star Trek'.

The face is still clearly me, and not the creation of a surgeon. The good Dr Neuprez has kept to her promise that she would make me look 10 years younger, but nothing too drastic. Her view is that people should notice that her patient is looking better, but not be certain why. I hope that happens with me.

This was the first time I'd been out since returning to London, and I really feel exhausted. I'd stayed in for two reasons. First, I looked pretty strange in that black hood, and there was no need to frighten the horses. Second, because the clinic believes that rest and sleep continues to be the best treatment for you even after those first 48 hours.

In a way it's been a bit of an anticlimax until today, nothing like the experience depicted in the books on cosmetic surgery, or the advice on websites. No pain of any seriousness. No desperate tiredness. No panic calls to the clinic.

I have to remind myself that mine was only a mini facelift, but that is all most men would ever consider. Were any of the scare stories true? Truthfully not, in my case. Equally I don't think the recovery time stories are true.

There is no way that you can expect to slide back into life after 10 days, which is what the guides tell you. I don't even have the stitches out until next Wednesday, which will be 12 days after the operation, and the swelling will not go down for several days after that.

If my experience is typical – and I've been let off easily – it takes a full fortnight out of your life, before you can rejoin the world.

OP + TWELVE DAYS

The stitches are out. Have just returned from Harley Street, where Dr Moraci removed the lot. Once again, no pain, no drama. Asked him how much skin was removed. He said it was about five centimetres each side. Two inches. Two inches of excess skin that had dropped over the last 20 years.

I have now finished the medical part of the project. Two weeks of my life gone on this project, £2,000 spent, and it looks like it's going to work.

OP + FIFTEEN DAYS

Went back to work today. Dr. Moraci saw no reason why I couldn't return to work, and he was right. Were there gasps of amazement or mocking insinuations? No. One said my holiday had done me good and I looked younger than when I left; another asked if I'd been to the dentist; one colleague said she was amazed by the difference in two weeks. She's going to guess, I thought, but then she asked if I had lost a lot of weight on holiday? So, no problems.

SIX MONTHS LATER

Have been trying to sum up what I would say right now if any friend asked me what I'd pass on from the experience. The points I would certainly include are:

- It's no big deal. Cosmetic surgery has changed enormously, even in the last five years. The techniques are better; the anaesthetics are better; the old horror stories belong to American TV. I can truthfully say that I suffered no real pain.

- It is difficult to know how to choose your surgeon, You may get a CV from them, but there are no guides as to their track record. You can check that they're on the right medical lists for this work; you can ask to see some examples of their work. But finally it's how you feel when you're with them. Do they listen to you? Do you trust them? Do you like them?

- It's important to check out the Clinic. Standards vary and so do prices. London is twice as dear as nearly every town in Europe. You may decide it's worth the extra money, but, when I checked, I found one London hospital charged £6,000 for a mini face lift and a three night stay, not including the surgeon or anaesthetist. I paid £1,900 with a one night stay, and that did include surgeon and anaesthetist.

- Every clinic gives you endless notes of advice on what to do before the op and after. Follow them. I've included most of them in my diary, and I think every bit of advice made the operation much easier.

- Forget the stories about being up and about in three days. I had the easiest of mini-face lifts, and yet I wasn't ready to rejoin the world for two weeks. You don't stay in bed, you can work happily at home, but your body does demand rest. Your face also is not ready for public viewing for at least 10 days, and better to wait a fortnight.

- One unexpected result. The sides of my face, where the skin was lifted, are still slightly numbed, and it still takes twice as long to get a good shave.

- Is it worth it? I think it is. I feel better, my wife can't believe it, colleagues and friends see nothing strange, simply someone who is looking better and younger.

- Last thought. I have that old puritan guilt at spending money on myself, but I am now very pleased that I indulged myself with a mini facelift. It may have cost nearly £2,000, but the long term effects are arguably better than any other indulgence I could imagine.

QUESTIONS

1. Would you ever consider cosmetic surgery? If so, what would be your main reason?

2. Where does it come in the hierarchy of potential indulgences for £2000, such as, for example, a long weekend at the Danieli in Venice, respray of the car, a Cartier Tank, lasik surgery for the eyes, two new bespoke suits, or a new wall plasma TV screen?

2. Do you think a mini face lift an act of sheer vanity, or a marvellous way to look younger?

"Eyes are the window to the soul."

Cicero

The Lasik Miracle

Does Laser Eye treatment work? It did for me. I had my eyes lasiked five years ago and have not needed glasses since

It's a game played from schooldays, isn't it? If you had to lose one of your senses, which would you choose? Most of us would probably give up the sense of touch first, then of taste, but then which? Hearing, speech, and, finally, sight was my order. Others were different and put speech before hearing, but everyone put sight as the last sense to lose.

Which is why I investigated a long time before having my eyes treated. I didn't <u>need</u> to have them lasered. I'd worn glasses since university for reading or working, and then gradually, over the years, needed them to drive, or simply see people clearly.

After a boring period of always having two sets of glasses for near and far sight, I graduated to varifocals, which was fine, except they cost a fortune for a couple of sets, as the eyes got worse. I tried contact lenses, but totally failed every time. My eyes are very dry, which didn't help, and so I was stuck with glasses.

Trouble was that I didn't enjoy wearing them. Nothing wrong with glasses, except that I was constantly losing mine. I tried not wearing them when out walking or running, but so many people accused me of cutting them dead, because I simply couldn't make out faces clearly enough to recognise them, that I had to wear them just to walk around.

My life changed when I was watching the Golf Masters from Augusta, and Peter Alliss started saying how much better someone was putting, now that they had had Lasik surgery.

Why, even the young Master himself, Tiger Woods, he said, had had his eyes lasiked, as well as Phil Mickelson, Ernie Els and a dozen other stars on the circuit.

The idea that I could walk down the street without glasses, that I could actually recognise someone across a room without glasses was promise enough, but that I might actually putt better was a promise that had to be explored.

I learnt that, by the miracles of medical science and technology, it is now possible for an experienced ophthalmic surgeon to reshape the corneas in your eyes, so as to remove any imperfections that are causing you to have short sight, long sight or astigmatism.

The most usual form of this treatment is called LASIK (which stands for Laser in Situ Keratomileusis), and takes no more than 10 minutes each eye.

Before you decide to have this treatment you need to go to a specialist Eye Clinic or hospital, where they will test your eyes to see if they can be treated successfully, and answer any questions you may have. If they decide that your eyes are going to respond to LASIK, and if you decide to go ahead, all the information from your tests is fed into the computer, to be programmed to supply the corneal changes needed by your eyes.

There is no pain, as anaesthetic drops are given you five minutes before you lie down and place your head beneath an advanced laser. The surgeon, with microsurgery, creates a thin flap on the eye, which is lifted back to allow the laser, using ultraviolet light, to reshape your cornea in a few seconds.

The surgeon then replaces the flap, which automatically heals itself over the next few days and weeks. You are given some antibiotic drops to prevent any infection, before you leave the theatre. You then sit down with your eyes closed for half an hour, before the surgeon checks that the operation has gone well.

You can then go home, clasping your supply of eye drops, and two transparent shields to wear over your eyes at night, to prevent you accidentally rubbing them. You wear these for two weeks when sleeping, and plain, non-prescription glasses when awake, to protect the eyes against dust. If your eyes are particularly sensitive, they recommend the glasses are tinted. Whichever you choose, the one thing you must never do is rub your eyes, which would obviously affect the healing of the lid.

You do not go swimming, have a shower, or wear eye make-up for a month, again for the obvious reason of keeping the eye totally protected. If you have dry eyes like me, then you will need to drop in some artificial tears several times a day.

Basically that's it, as far as we patients are concerned. It is the most undramatic operation anyone of us will probably have. No pain: no bandages: no blood; no long period of convalescing.

It is quite simply a miracle. Suddenly, the world is clear. It is the most dramatic for those who were short-sighted, and maybe never saw the trees clearly or could pick out a bird singing in the garden. But it was dramatic enough for long-sighted people, like me, who could see a distant tree clearly, but not the person across the table.

My eyes felt a little rough the first evening, but next morning that had gone, and I worked gently for a few hours, before cycling back to the clinic for the check-up that they insist on within 24 hours. The surgeon pronounced that he was very happy with both eyes. Next day I drove the car without any problems. I was given a 24 hour emergency number to ring, but never used it. They insist on seeing you again a week after the treatment, then after six weeks, six months and so on.

If someone had suggested having my eyes lasiked 20 years ago, I would have refused. There wasn't enough history to prove it worked. Now there is.

In 1995 the US Government's tough Food & Drug Administration finally gave its seal of approval, calling LASIK *safe and effective.* Since then around a million Americans a year have had this treatment, and another million people are treated annually in some 30 countries.

In the UK, LASIK is only beginning to be understood, and we do only about 25,000 laser treatments a year. Nearly half of these are carried out in clinics run by *Ultralase,* which is where I went. They did a first-class job on me, but there are other Clinics, including one at *Moorfields Hospital,* and the costs vary from

£2,000 upwards for both eyes, including all follow-up consultation and treatment. All the Clinics have web sites with a mass of information.

I suspect that eye laser treatment will become as normal in a few years as, for example, having the appendix out is now. I know of no surgery that can be as painless, yet produce such a miracle.

QUESTIONS

1. When would you consider lasik?

2. How high a priority does it come in your Grand Plan?

3. Or does the whole idea terrify you?

Useful Web Sites

Charities
ageconcern.co.uk
helptheaged.org.uk

Employment
efa.org.uk
taen.org.uk
dti.gov/er/equality/age

Pensions Advisory Services
opas.org.uk
thepensionservice.gov.uk

Property & Lifetime Mortgages
ship-ltd. org
nationwide.co.uk
keyrs.co.uk
halifax.co.uk
arla.co.uk

Medical
prostate-cancer.org.uk
realage.co.uk
livingTo100.com
baaps.org.uk
elyzea.co.uk
ultralase.co.uk
bhf.org.uk

Over 50s web sites
saga.co.uk
seniority.co.uk
arpO50.org.uk
over50s.com
laterlife.com
silversurfers.net
revolutionizeretirement.com

Financial Information
fsa.gov.uk
fool.co.uk
moneysupermarket.com
moneySavingExpert.com
thisismoney.co.uk
datamonitor.com

Financial Advisors
hargreaveslansdown.co.uk
annuity-bureau.co.uk.
annuitydirect.co.uk
dwcifa.com

Home Services Comparisons
uSwitch.co.uk
simplyswitch.com
skype.com
dialaphone.co.uk

The Silver Wolf A to Z Guide to Your Third Act

Your First Act is your education for some 20 years. Your Second Act is your time for hard work, making your way in the world for some 35 years. Your Third Act, from the mid-fifties to your late-seventies, is the time you make your own life. These can be the best 25 years of your life, but they may need a change of attitude. Check out the *Silver Wolf* A–Z guide to your Third Act.

A is for **Adventure**. The Third Act is the greatest adventure of your life. These years are when you make your dreams come true. Only you know what they are; now is the time to start the Grand Plan to achieve them.

B is for **Be yourself**. Know Yourself. The oldest advice in the world, but still the best. The Third Act is the time to be honest about who you are and what you want to achieve in your lifetime.

C is for **Carpe Diem**. Seize the day, the Romans taught. You may have 20 years to carry out your Grand Plan, but that's only 7,300 days. No time for procrastination.

D is for **Dreams**. You've had these for years, but in the maelstrom of the earlier years, there never seemed time. Now there is. As you begin to change the pattern of your life, make room for all the dreams and hopes that you ever had.

E is for **Exercise**. Run up and down stairs, walk a mile, have energetic sex for 30 minutes. Do whatever you like, but exercise your body. The deal with your body is this. You exercise it daily, give it the right food it needs, and don't fill it with nicotine and too much alcohol. In return, it will keep you healthy.

F is for Fun. Remember the fun times? It's time to have them again. Make having fun an integral part of your plan, and enjoy every day.

G is for the Grand Plan. This is your blueprint for your Third Act. Write your personal mission statement for the great adventure, and lay out your Grand Plan for the next 25 years. What you want to achieve, how you will do it, when you will do it, and why. Your Grand Plan is the most important project of your life.

H is for Home. The right home in the right place is at the heart of your Third Act. Choose the home that's best for your life, not others; and use its value, when you need more money to fund your Grand Plan.

I is for Illness. Contrary to myth, these are not decades of health problems. Look after your body and you may have less problems than you did in middle-age.

J is for Join In. Be part of life; don't stay on the edge of the circle, always the spectator. Leave the audience seats, and become the star on stage.

K is for Knowledge. Learn something new every day. It's another myth that you can't teach an old dog new tricks. You can often learn at 60 better than you did at 30. Enjoy the challenge of learning and the joy of achievement.

L is for Laughter. Laugh often and aloud; don't just smile. Laughter makes the world a better place, and does wonders for your health.

M **is for Manage Your Money**. Money isn't going to buy you happiness in any decade, but your Third Act is no time to have money worries. Do your long term budgets, and set down financial plans to meet your needs. Remember the inevitable effect of inflation.

N **is for Nourishing**. Nourish your relationships with your family, friends and colleagues. Give more of yourself to them. Throw away any veneer of cynicism you wore in your Second Act; it's time to be true to your beliefs and uphold your values.

O **is for Old**. Which you are not. You are simply older than some, younger than others. The bonus is that you are also more knowledgeable, more experienced, more tolerant, and more mature.

P **is for Pension.** It could be P for pennies, after successive governments have stolen our money, but it's not too late to make new plans for the next two decades.

Q **is for Quality of Life**. You deserve it, take it. Downsize your life, throw out things that just fill your space, and any thoughts that just fill your mind. The Third Act is about quality, not quantity.

R **is for Retire**. Which you will never do. You will never retire from life or work. The old form of retirement was a state of mind that rarely led to happiness, and has no part in your Grand Plan. You are not retiring; you are just beginning a new life.

S **is for Sex.** Good at any age, better in the Third Act. Good for your health, your longevity and your eyes. Enjoy!

T **is for Togetherness**. The Third Act is the beginning of a new kind of togetherness with your partner at home. You need to work out what each wants and expects, as your lives begin to change, If you are alone, decide what kind of future partnership you need.

U is for Unique. Your Third Act will be unique, because only you create your Grand Plan, and only you will carry it out. Others will have their dreams and plans, but none will be the same as yours.

V is for Vote. There are 20 million people over 50 and you can decide on which party gets into power. Use your vote only for those who promise the reforms we need, and, in particular, make ageism as unacceptable as racism or sexism.

W is for Work. Work for money, for charity, for the Third World, anything, but keep working. Certainly not for five days a week, but make some work as part of your Plan. All play and no work is not much fun.

X is for Excess Weight. If you have it, get rid of it. Obesity is the greatest destroyer of a happy and long Third Act. Eat less, eat slowly, eat nothing on the move, and eat nothing, bar fruit, that can be eaten without utensils. Drink more water, less alcohol, and try to like green tea.

Y is for Young. You are young. You have all the youthful enthusiasm of starting a new life, and, while ageism lingers on, it helps to keep looking young. If Nature isn't helping you, then science can.

Z is for Zeal. Be zealous about living. Show your enthusiasm, be generous in your praise, see the glass as always half full. Enjoy the fulfilment of your dreams, and enhance the life of others.

dp

Also available from Delancey Press

☐ Have I Ever Told You…	Larry Adler	£ 9.95
☐ Sensual Pleasures	Sally Farmiloe-Neville	£ 16.99
and the Art of Morphing into a Health Goddess		
☐ Morgan's Castle	Jane Huxley	£ 14.95
☐ For the Love of Penny Whistler	Jane Huxley	£ 14.95
☐ Chip Donovan and the Dragonfly	Bill Russell	£ 8.50

DELANCEY PRESS, 23 Berkeley Square, London W1J 6HE
Phone: 020 7665 6605   Email: delanceypress@aol.com

☐ I enclose a UK cheque or Postal Order payable to Delancey Press for

£ ………………

☐ Please charge £ ……………… to my Access, Mastercard, Visa, Delta or
Switch card no.

☐☐☐☐☐☐☐☐☐☐☐☐☐☐☐☐☐☐

Expiry Date ☐☐ ☐☐   Switch Issue No. ☐☐☐

Delivery – UK: free
Europe: add 25% of retail price
Rest of the world: add 40% of retail price
Please allow 14 days for delivery within the UK. Offer subject to price and availability.

NAME (block letters please)

……………………………………………………………………………………

ADDRESS ……………………………………………………………………………

……………………………………………………………………………………

……………………………………………………………………………………

Postcode ………………………………   Telephone …………………………………

Email ………………………………………………………………………………

Signature …………………………………………